JUN 1 3

PARANORMAL FILES
BIGFOOT AND OTHER APE-MEN

Stuart Webb

ROSEN
PUBLISHING®
New York

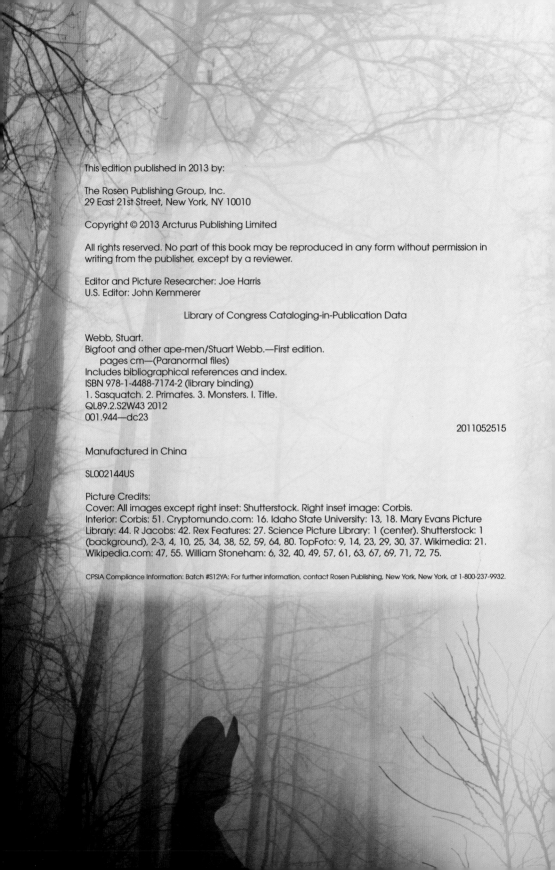

This edition published in 2013 by:

The Rosen Publishing Group, Inc.
29 East 21st Street, New York, NY 10010

Editor and Picture Researcher: Joe Harris
U.S. Editor: John Kemmerer

Library of Congress Cataloging-in-Publication Data

Webb, Stuart.
Bigfoot and other ape-men/Stuart Webb.—First edition.
    pages cm—(Paranormal files)
Includes bibliographical references and index.
ISBN 978-1-4488-7174-2 (library binding)
1. Sasquatch. 2. Primates. 3. Monsters. I. Title.
QL89.2.S2W43 2012
001.944—dc23

                                                                    2011052515

Manufactured in China

SL002144US

Picture Credits:
Cover: All images except right inset: Shutterstock. Right inset image: Corbis.
Interior: Corbis: 51. Cryptomundo.com: 16. Idaho State University: 13, 18. Mary Evans Picture Library: 44. R Jacobs: 42. Rex Features: 27. Science Picture Library: 1 (center). Shutterstock: 1 (background), 2-3, 4, 10, 25, 34, 38, 52, 59, 64, 80. TopFoto: 9, 14, 23, 29, 30, 37. Wikimedia: 21. Wikipedia.com: 47, 55. William Stoneham: 6, 32, 40, 49, 57, 61, 63, 67, 69, 71, 72, 75.

CPSIA Compliance Information: Batch #S12YA: For further information, contact Rosen Publishing, New York, New York, at 1-800-237-9932.

CONTENTS

Bigfoot: First Impressions 4

Bigfoot: Hitting the Headlines 12

Bigfoot: Filming a Sasquatch.............................. 20

Bigfoot: Assessing the Evidence 28

The Skunk Ape 36

The Yeti.. 44

The Maricoxi 52

Asian Wild Men.. 58

Orang Pendek 66

The Australian Yowie 70

Glossary 76

Further Information 78

Index.. 79

BIGFOOT: FIRST IMPRESSIONS

The native peoples of North America are the source of the oldest stories about Bigfoot, or Sasquatch. Each tribe had its own name for it. They called it *wendigo, chenoo,* or *kiwakwe*. They all described a creature covered in fur that looked like a very large human and lived in remote forested areas. As early as 1793, European settlers in North America were reporting sightings of a "hairy ape-man." A legend soon grew up of a "wild man of the woods," and there were several newspaper reports of scary encounters by hunters and trappers during the 19th and early 20th centuries.

The Battle of Ape Canyon

Then, in 1924, the *Oregonian* newspaper from Portland, Oregon, carried a story that was unlike the others. The report related the account of five gold prospectors who had been panning for gold around the Lewis River, close to Mount St. Helens. The prospectors – Fred Beck, Marion Smith, Roy Smith, Gabe Lafever, and John Peterson – had been working their claim for over two years by the time of the alleged encounter.

Could the forests around Mount St. Helens be home to the Sasquatch?

According to the men, one afternoon in July 1924, they began to hear a noise as if somebody was banging loudly on a hollow wooden trunk. This was followed by a loud whistling call coming from a wooded ridge that overlooked their camp. After a week of this, the men habitually carried their rifles with them when collecting firewood or water.

One day, Marion Smith and Fred Beck were fetching water when – so they later claimed – they saw one of the "mountain gorillas" about 300 ft (91 m) away. It stood about 7 ft (213 cm) tall on its hind legs, and it was watching the two men from behind a pine tree. Smith fired three shots but only hit the tree, so the creature ran off uninjured. When it reappeared from the trees, now about 600 ft (183 m) away, Beck fired but missed. They ran back to the cabin to consult with the others. Faced by gigantic man-like creatures, the prospectors decided to depart. However, it was getting late in the day, so they decided to stay the night rather than risk being caught in the woods in the dark with the "mountain gorillas."

Midnight Attack

At midnight, the men later alleged, they were awoken by a terrific thump as something hit the cabin wall. The sound of heavy footfalls came from outside the cabin, and Smith peered out through a chink between the logs to see three of the huge creatures. It also sounded as if there were others nearby. The creatures then picked up large rocks with which they began to pound at the walls. The men grabbed their guns and prepared to face the beasts if they should break in.

According to the men, at least two of the apes got onto the roof and began jumping up and down. Another began pounding on the door, which Beck braced shut with a wooden pole. After several terrifying minutes, the assault ended and the creatures slipped away into the darkness. But less than an hour later they were back. Again they attacked the cabin, trying to break in, and again they retreated, only to return with redoubled fury to the assault.

APE-MAN FILE

CRYPTIDS

A cryptid is a creature whose existence is claimed in stories or legends, but which is not recognized by science. Bigfoot, and the other creatures described in this book, are all apelike cryptids. Do they exist? Scientists argue that eyewitness reports, however numerous or credible, are not sufficient evidence to prove a creature exists. They point to the fact that witnesses might mistake a sighting of one creature for something else, or be the victims of hoaxes. What is needed is hard evidence, such as a body, that can be independently analyzed and verified.

Yowie

Orange Pendak

Yeren

Yeti

Maricoxi

Wildman

Falling over the edge of a canyon, it dropped 400 ft (122 m) to the rocks below.

When they got to Spirit Lake, the men reported their experience to the local rangers. The story soon got out, and a team of armed reporters hurried up into the hills to find the cabin. Although some days had passed, the signs of the assault were still to be seen and the cabin was surrounded by gigantic footprints – some of which were ominously fresh. The reporters, like the miners, got out quickly. The place was dubbed Ape Canyon by the press, and it is known by that name to this day.

Ostman's Encounter

Soon after the newspapers carried the story of the Battle of Ape Canyon, rumors spread through the area that

Finally, as dawn broke, the creatures left. After a while, the terrified miners gingerly opened the door and peered outside. All was quiet. They packed up and set off with as much as they could carry, leaving behind over $200 worth of equipment. As they set off down the trail toward civilization, the men saw one of the creatures emerge from the trees just 80 yards (73 meters) away. Beck whipped out his rifle and fired. This time he did not miss. The creature collapsed.

"a young Swede" had been kidnapped by the "mountain gorillas" and that he had lived with his captors for some time. The "young Swede" turned out to be a Canadian of Swedish extraction named Albert Ostman.

In the summer of 1924, Ostman was working on a construction site in British Columbia. He decided to take a break and went up into the mountains to look for one of the many small gold deposits that exist in that region. He camped out with just a sleeping bag, rather than a tent, because the weather was warm. When he returned to camp one night, he noticed that his things had been disturbed, as if somebody had been rummaging through them. Blaming animals looking for food, Ostman decided to tuck his rifle into his sleeping bag so that it would be handy in case a bear appeared.

According to Ostman, he was awoken during the night by being pushed roughly down into his sleeping bag, which was then picked up and thrown over something. Ostman's first thought was that he had been thrown over a horse by bandits. Then he realized that the movement of the thing carrying him was not like that of a horse, but more like a man.

Ostman felt a second bag filled with cans and equipment bumping against him and deduced that his captor had also grabbed his sealed bag of supplies. After a while, Ostman felt that they were going up a steep hill. Then they began to go downhill, at which point the sleeping bag was dumped on the ground and dragged along for a while. It was again picked up and carried, but, after about three hours of this, it was dropped onto the ground for the last time. It rolled downhill for a short distance and then stopped, and Ostman could hear what sounded like chattering and grunting.

TALE OF THE PARANORMAL

MUCHALAT HARRY

Four years after Ostman's encounter, another man claimed to be the victim of a similar kind of kidnapping. Muchalat Harry was a fur trapper from Vancouver Island who said he was taken from his camp one night and found himself captured by around twenty Sasquatch. Seeing a pile of gnawed bones nearby, he became terrified that he would be eaten. He managed to escape to tell his tale.

Captured by Ape-Men

Cautiously he poked his head out of the sleeping bag. At first he could see little because it was dark, but as the dawn came up he could gradually distinguish four huge figures. Ostman later described them as massively muscled, hairy apelike men. There was, he said, a large male, who was clearly the leader, an equally large female, and two smaller figures, one male and one female. Ostman guessed that he was seeing the mountain ape-men that the local Indians had told him about and that he had been captured by a family group.

Recovering from his shock, Ostman reasoned that the creature who had brought him here must have had plenty of opportunity to kill him if it had wanted to do so. He looked around and saw that they were in a small area of about 7 acres (28,328 sq m) surrounded by sheer rocks, which had only one visible opening. The older male sat there as if keeping watch. Realizing that he was being left alone, Ostman set out to explore the area. He found a source of water, emptied his sack of stores, and set up camp, all the time watching for an opportunity to escape.

As Ostman later described it, the younger creatures at first seemed frightened of him, but by the end of the first day they appeared more accepting. Ostman rolled an empty snuff box toward the young male, who picked up the shiny object with interest. When he found out how to open and close the box, the young male delightedly took it to the young female and showed her. Then he went to the older male and sat chattering to him for some time.

Apart from being offered some roots and leaves to eat, Ostman was ignored, but when he tried to leave, the older male blocked his way and glared at him. He considered shooting his way out, but he only had six bullets and did not think that this would be enough to kill four such massive animals.

Studying the Creatures

Ostman later claimed that he camped out with his kidnappers for several days, which gave him plenty of time to study them and their behavior. The two larger creatures were over 7 ft (213 cm) tall, the younger ones around 6 ft (183 cm). All of them were massively built, with huge barrel chests of up to 55 in (137 cm) and waists of 40 in (101 cm).

Ostman guessed their weight at over 600 lb (272 kg). Their heads, he later said, were flat-faced, like those of humans, but were small in relation to their bodies, and they met the body without a noticeable neck. They had low foreheads that sloped up to a peak at the rear, although some of this was made up of stiff hair. Their teeth were big and strong, and, although the older male had enlarged incisors, they were not big enough to be called tusks.

TALE OF THE PARANORMAL
THE RUBY CREEK INCIDENT

George and Jennie Chapman and their three children lived near the village of Ruby Creek, British Columbia. During the summer of 1941, while George was away working, the eldest son and Jennie claimed they spotted a gigantic man, covered in hair, near their house. When it saw them, it uttered a cry and began striding toward them. Alarmed, Jennie sent her boy back into the house. She then shepherded her children out of the house, hidden under a blanket, hoping the Sasquatch wouldn't see them. They fled to Ruby Creek.

When George arrived home two hours later, he found the door to the outhouse smashed in, food scattered about and half eaten, and giant footprints in the soil. It was with relief that he found his family safe at Jennie's father's house in Ruby Creek. On five more nights after that, the family heard the cry of the Sasquatch and found footprints near their house.

After the Bigfoot encounter, the Chapmans abandoned their wooden cabin, and it fell into disrepair.

Heavily muscled arms, longer in proportion than a human's, ended in large hands with short and stubby fingers that had fingernails like chisels. Their feet were massive, and the soles were heavily padded, like the pads on a dog's feet, but otherwise they were like those of a human.

According to Ostman, the creatures were active both by day and by night. They slept on what he described as blankets – sheets of woven bark and moss. Each day one or two of the creatures left in search of food, bringing back grass, roots, and leaves – Ostman did not see them eat meat of any kind. When they were not out looking for food, the two older creatures rested. The younger ones, by contrast, would play games and horse around. The male had a game in which he would hold his feet in his hands and then bounce along on his backside, as if seeing how far he could get without touching the ground with any of his limbs.

After several days of this, Ostman got a small fire going and brewed himself some coffee. The smell attracted the two males, who came and sat down about 10 ft (305 cm) from him. Ostman poured himself some coffee and spread butter on some biscuits, and the two creatures watched him carefully as he ate and drank. When he had finished his meal, Ostman opened a new snuff box and took a pinch.

Bigfoot is often described as a giant hairy man.

The older male then reached forward, took the box, and emptied the entire contents into his mouth.

Escape

A few seconds later he began to squeal and claw at his tongue. He rolled over, then leapt up and dashed for the spring to drink some water. The other creatures went after him as if they were worried. Two thoughts immediately occurred to Ostman. Firstly, the old male, once he'd recovered, might become dangerously angry. And secondly, the exit from the little valley was unguarded for the first time since he had arrived. Ostman grabbed his rifle and his bag of supplies and raced for the exit. He was almost there when he heard footsteps behind him. He looked over his shoulder to see the older female running toward him. Dropping his bag, Ostman turned and fired a shot over her head. The female stopped instantly and bolted in the other direction.

Grabbing his bag again, Ostman ran out of the valley and continued for over 1 mile (1.6 km) before he paused. He then scrambled up a slope so that he could look back toward his captors. There was no sign of pursuit, but even so he decided to take no chances. He walked all day, stopping only to shoot and cook a grouse before moving on. Two days later he stumbled across a small group of lumberjacks who took him in and gave him a meal before

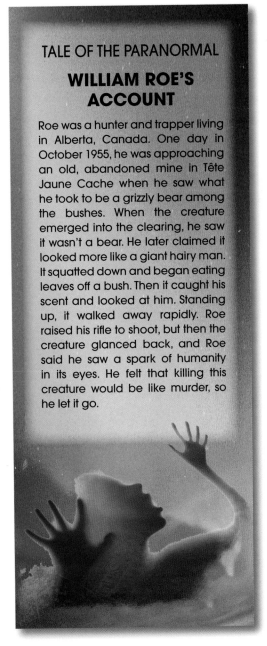

TALE OF THE PARANORMAL

WILLIAM ROE'S ACCOUNT

Roe was a hunter and trapper living in Alberta, Canada. One day in October 1955, he was approaching an old, abandoned mine in Tête Jaune Cache when he saw what he took to be a grizzly bear among the bushes. When the creature emerged into the clearing, he saw it wasn't a bear. He later claimed it looked more like a giant hairy man. It squatted down and began eating leaves off a bush. Then it caught his scent and looked at him. Standing up, it walked away rapidly. Roe raised his rifle to shoot, but then the creature glanced back, and Roe said he saw a spark of humanity in its eyes. He felt that killing this creature would be like murder, so he let it go.

driving him down to their base camp. From there Ostman was able to make his way to Vancouver. He never went prospecting in the mountains again.

BIGFOOT: HITTING THE HEADLINES

The modern Bigfoot legend began in 1958, sparked by events at Bluff Creek in northern California. A road was being built through the area to aid the logging industry by opening the region up to heavy machinery. Ray Wallace was the head of the firm hired to do the job. His brother Wilbur was one of the foremen in charge of the task of clearing a flat roadbed through the rugged and densely forested terrain.

Nocturnal Intruder

On August 3, 1958, the workmen on the Bluff Creek road turned up for work to find some of their equipment disturbed. A spare tire weighing around 700 lb (317 kg) had been rolled about, causing the men to wonder who or what had been interfering. On August 27, the workmen discovered that the site had again been visited by something overnight, and this time it had left footprints.

Jerry Crew found them. They were impressed into the soft soil around his bulldozer. The footprints were later described as being exactly like those of a naked human foot, but much larger. At first Crew thought that someone was playing a practical joke, but after following the tracks and studying them more closely, he became convinced that they had really been left by a huge man of some kind. He went to see his foreman, Wilbur Wallace, who looked at the tracks. After some discussion, it was decided to ignore the strange nocturnal intruder – as long as he did not turn up in daylight hours when the work crew were on site.

On September 21, the local newspaper, the *Humboldt Times*, printed a letter from Mrs. Jesse Bemis, the wife of one of the workmen on the site, about the events up at Bluff Creek. Reporter Betty Allen then made the link between the mysterious giant footprints and the stories that had been circulating for years about a hairy man-ape that the local settlers and farmers called "Big Foot." Allen went out to talk to people who had actually seen the tracks of the man-ape. On September 28, she had a piece published about the creature she called "Bigfoot," which summarized the evidence to date. She also suggested

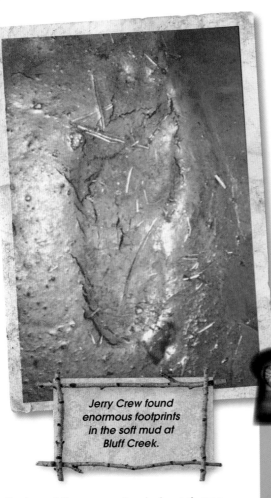

Jerry Crew found enormous footprints in the soft mud at Bluff Creek.

of Paris and instructions on how to use it. On October 3, Titmus arrived at the worksite and, together with Crew, poured the plaster into the clearest of the footprints. Crew took the cast down to the offices of the *Humboldt Times.* He and the cast were photographed and the photo was used to illustrate an article by the newspaper's editor Andrew Genzoli. The story was taken up and reprinted across the USA and Canada, and then the rest of the world. A legend was born.

that next time somebody found any footprints, they should take a cast using plaster of Paris.

Plaster Cast

On October 1, the Bluff Creek work gang found more footprints that had been left overnight around their worksite. Two of the workers promptly quit. Wilbur Wallace asked his brother and boss, Ray Wallace, to come up to Bluff Creek to go over the situation.

Meanwhile, Jerry Crew called an old friend of his, Bob Titmus, who went to see Betty Allen to get some plaster

EYEWITNESS ACCOUNT

CLEAR, DEEP FOOTPRINTS

This is an excerpt from Betty Allen's first article about Bigfoot, published on September 28, 1958. The article includes the first use of the word "bigfoot" in print to describe the Sasquatch. It acquired its capital letter later.

"What did we expect to see? Maybe one track and we could say it was all a hoax.... Jerry Crew directed us to the location of the tracks.

"'I'll show you those tracks,' Crew said. I could tell that some of the construction men were quite skeptical. I am told that some of them wouldn't even go and take a look.

"The first actual line of tracks definitely jolted me! On the hard ground where Philip Ammon's (Allen's colleague) number 12's made a very light imprint, the track of bigfoot sunk a half to three quarters of an inch (127–190 mm) in depth. Twenty clear deep footprints marched along the side of the traveled portion of the road. Eighteen more were seen at intervals where the tractors had not run over them."

Back at Bluff Creek, the excitement mounted when, on October 12, two workers – Ray Kerr and Bob Breazle – claimed they actually saw the mysterious footprint-maker. According to them, they were driving along a local dirt road after dark when they momentarily caught a gigantic upright figure in their headlights. The creature ran off into the woods. The men described it as a hairy human figure well over 6 ft (183 cm) tall. Within 48 hours another 13 men had left their jobs on the road construction project.

Newspaper reports of the events around Bluff Creek attracted two Yeti investigators, John Green and René Dahinden. These men were in touch with a Texas millionaire named Tom Slick whose interest in mystery animals and other odd phenomena made him willing to invest money in research.

Meanwhile, Bob Titmus was out in the forests looking for signs of the mysterious creature. So far as is known, he was the first man ever to go looking for Sasquatch. He found some more footprints and took casts.

Titmus, Green, and Dahinden would all devote huge amounts of time and effort to the search for the mystery creature. Between them they amassed a vast number of footprint casts, eyewitness accounts, hair samples, and other evidence. Also on the scene

This photographer is measuring a Bluff Creek footprint before taking a picture.

Ape-man File

DID RAY WALLACE FAKE ALL THE BLUFF CREEK FOOTPRINTS?

Skeptics believe that practical joker Wallace was responsible for all the footprints found at Bluff Creek, including the original ones found by Jerry Crew. They allege that Wallace's company was falling behind with its work and Wallace needed a reason to extend the deadline. On the other hand, Wallace was away from the state on business when at least some of the tracks appeared. Believers in the Sasquatch are more inclined to the view that Wallace took to his hoaxing as a result of events in Bluff Creek, which he then set out to exploit.

fairly quickly was the zoologist Ivan T. Sanderson, who was writing a book about North American ecology.

A character destined to play a more controversial role in the story was Ray Wallace, the head of the road construction company. Wallace later admitted owning a pair of gigantic wooden feet with which he went about faking Bigfoot tracks. He also claimed to have photographed and filmed Bigfoot on several occasions. On another occasion he said that he had killed one of the creatures and had hidden its body away. He never

actually produced the photos, film, or body for inspection.

After his death in 2002, one of his relatives went so far as to claim that Wallace had "invented Bigfoot" and that he had been responsible for nearly all the evidence that supported the idea that a giant man-ape existed in the Pacific Northwest. "The reality is that Bigfoot just died," the newspapers announced after Wallace's death.

Reports Multiply

Following the Bluff Creek episode, stories of Bigfoot encounters came flooding in. In the summer of 1959, a Mrs. Bellevue was startled by a humanlike ape with reddish hair watching her from behind some trees while she was camping in British Columbia.

In August 1961, John Bringsli was out picking huckleberries near Nelson, British Columbia. After parking his car, he wandered off into the woods with a basket. He did not hear anything, but on looking up he claims he saw a Sasquatch walking hesitatingly and slowly toward him. The creature stood about 8 ft (244 cm) tall and was covered in greyish hair. At a distance of less than 50 ft (15 m), the two looked at each other for a moment in silence, then Bringsli fled for his car. The last time he saw the Sasquatch, it was still close to the huckleberry bush, wearing an expression of mild curiosity as it watched him leave.

A Sighting with Tracks

In July 1963, on the Lewis River, near its confluence with the Columbia River in Oregon, another Sasquatch was allegedly seen. The witnesses, Mr. and Mrs. Martin Hennrich, claim they were spotted by the creature, which fled into some woodland. They reported the event to the local press, and the story was noticed by researcher John Green. He hurried to the scene and was able to take plaster casts of the 16-in (41-cm) tracks that had been left behind by the creature. This was one of the very first times that casts had been taken of footprints that could be linked to a reported sighting of a Sasquatch. Previously, when Sasquatch were seen it had either been on hard ground or it had rained soon afterward and

This photograph of "Bigfoot" was taken by a backpacker on November 17, 2005.

spoiled any prints that might have been made. This combined sighting and footprint casting seemed to confirm that the two phenomena – footprints and sightings of giant humanlike creatures – were aspects of the same enigma.

Sasquatch and Dogs

A number of reports made in the early 1960s seemed to suggest that the relationship between Sasquatch and dogs was one of mutual dislike. One evening in the spring of 1963, at Toppenish in Washington State, a woman heard her guard dogs barking first in alarm and then in fear. The woman peered out of the window to see what was going on. She later claimed she saw a huge, apelike face peering back at her. The Sasquatch seemed to be just as surprised as she was because it fled.

In July of the same year, a Sasquatch reportedly approached the home of Gladys Herrarra, an isolated house near Satus Pass, Washington. Again, the first sign of anything unusual was the frenzied and terrified behavior of Herrarra's pet dog.

In October 1966, the Corey homestead near Yakima, Washington, was allegedly visited by a Sasquatch. The family dog attacked it, but the Sasquatch simply slapped it aside. When Mike Corey emerged from his house, the Sasquatch made off into the woods. Two days later, the dog's body was found. It had been savagely beaten to death.

TALE OF THE PARANORMAL

CHASED BY A SASQUATCH

In 1961, a Mr. Larry Martin reported a dramatic confrontation with a Sasquatch in the wooded hills above Alpine, Oregon. He had gone into the woods early one evening to help a friend retrieve a deer that he had shot. The two men drove up a dirt track to a spot close to the kill, then set off on foot. When they reached the spot where the deer should have been, it had gone. A clear drag mark led toward a patch of dense undergrowth. Intrigued, the two men followed. As Martin entered the bushes they were suddenly shaken with great violence by unseen hands.

At that moment, according to Martin, a large creature came into view – it was only a few yards away. It was, Martin later reported, about 7 ft (213 cm) tall, standing upright, with the head and face of a gorilla. He screamed and fled, rapidly followed by his friend. The Sasquatch gave chase with long, loping strides that thumped the ground, but the two men leapt into the car, started the engine, and raced off. As he glanced in the rearview mirror, Martin saw the Sasquatch standing there in the road watching them go.

Farm Encounter

In June 1961, a dramatic encounter with a Sasquatch was reported by Robert Hatfield, a farmer living near Fort Bragg, California. Late one evening, the farm dogs began barking loudly. Hatfield went out onto his front porch to investigate and – so he later claimed – he saw a hairy head peering over the 6-ft (183-cm) high fence that surrounded the yard. Thinking it was a large bear, he went back into the house to fetch his brother-in-law Bud Jenkins, who happened to be staying over.

Jenkins fetched a flashlight and a rifle while his wife (Hatfield's sister) peered out into the darkness. Hatfield went back out into the yard. Hearing a noise from around the corner of the house, he went to investigate and almost bumped into what he later described as a hair-covered humanlike figure standing almost 8 ft (244 cm) tall. Hatfield fled, tripped, and continued on his hands and knees. He dashed into the house at top speed, screaming at his sister to shut the door. She went to close the door, but it jammed while still slightly ajar. Something was holding it open with great force. By this time, Jenkins had found his rifle and was stepping past the terrified Hatfield.

"Let it through," he told his wife. "I'll get it." He raised his rifle into the

This image captured by a hidden camera supposedly shows a Bigfoot eating red fir tree bark in Moyie Springs, northern Idaho.

shooting position and prepared to fire at whatever it was that was pushing against the door. As the woman hesitated, the door suddenly went slack. She slammed it shut and bolted it. Jenkins then walked to the window to peer into the darkness. He saw a humanlike figure striding off. It stepped over a 3-ft (91-cm) high fence without pausing and then faded into the gloom.

Watcher in the Trees

In August 1961, a woman identified only as Mrs. Calhoun was prospecting with her daughter near Quesnel, British Columbia. The pair had found a stream that seemed to be a likely spot for panning and the daughter had gone back to the car to fetch a packed lunch. According to Mrs. Calhoun's later report, she heard a noise and glanced round to see a creature watching her from the fringes of the forest that grew next to the stream. The beast, she said, was human in appearance, though its arms were too long in proportion to its body and it was covered in pale brown hair. Its head and shoulders were covered in longer, densely matted hair, and the top of its head sloped up and back to a point, while the nose was broad and flat. Mrs. Calhoun swung her rifle up to her shoulder and covered the beast as she began to edge along the stream toward her car. The creature watched her for a few seconds, then stepped back into the undergrowth and slipped out of sight.

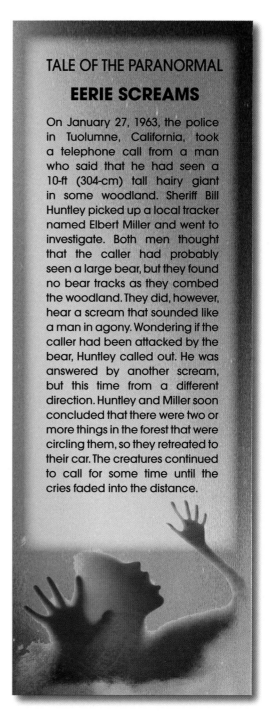

TALE OF THE PARANORMAL

EERIE SCREAMS

On January 27, 1963, the police in Tuolumne, California, took a telephone call from a man who said that he had seen a 10-ft (304-cm) tall hairy giant in some woodland. Sheriff Bill Huntley picked up a local tracker named Elbert Miller and went to investigate. Both men thought that the caller had probably seen a large bear, but they found no bear tracks as they combed the woodland. They did, however, hear a scream that sounded like a man in agony. Wondering if the caller had been attacked by the bear, Huntley called out. He was answered by another scream, but this time from a different direction. Huntley and Miller soon concluded that there were two or more things in the forest that were circling them, so they retreated to their car. The creatures continued to call for some time until the cries faded into the distance.

BIGFOOT: FILMING A SASQUATCH

The short cine film shot by Roger Patterson October 20, 1967, in Bluff Creek, northern California, remains the most important single piece of evidence for the existence of Bigfoot. The film is not without controversy. Patterson and his companion, Bob Gimlin, have been hailed as heroes by some, but condemned by others as frauds or victims of a hoax.

The Tip-Off

Patterson was a part-time rodeo rider who was interested in the Bigfoot legend and wanted to try to capture one on film. In early October 1967, Patterson got a call from one of his contacts in the growing community of Sasquatch investigators, a man from Willow Creek, California, called Al Hodgson. He told Patterson that some excellent new tracks had been found in the Blue Creek Mountain area. They were being studied by John Green and René Dahinden (see page 14). It was thought that one set of very large footprints had been made by a big male, a smaller set of footprints by a female, and a third, much smaller set of prints by a juvenile.

Patterson contacted his friend and fellow rodeo rider, Bob Gimlin, who agreed to join him in his search for the Sasquatch. The pair arrived in the area on October 6, by which time heavy rains had washed away the tracks that Patterson had hoped to film. They decided to stay, though, having come prepared for a two-week visit. Over the following days, the pair would drive to a likely area, make camp, and then spend the day riding about looking for footprints or other signs of Sasquatch.

Encounter in a Canyon

On October 20, they decided to explore a particularly rugged and remote region centered around a canyon. Patterson rode in front and Gimlin followed up behind, leading the packhorse. Both men were armed, and Patterson had the movie-camera in his saddlebag. What follows is their account of events.

They had been riding for some hours when they reached a pile of fallen trees and broken logs that had been deposited there by a flood in 1964. The obstruction blocked their view up the canyon. According to the two men, as they came around the log jam they

This famous image from the Patterson film shows the Bigfoot glancing behind it.

the canyon. Patterson got the camera working and yelled out, "Cover me," to Gimlin. At this, Gimlin pulled out his rifle, thereby letting go of the packhorse, which headed off downstream after Patterson's mount.

The Filming

Patterson was now running forward with the camera to his eye, trying to keep the Sasquatch in shot. He did not see a sudden rise in the ground, so he tripped and fell. The Sasquatch turned to stare at him. Fearing the creature might attack, Gimlin rode over to the creek, dismounted, and aimed his rifle at the Sasquatch, now only about 60 ft (18 m) away.

saw a Sasquatch beside the creek, about 80 ft (24.5 m) from them. The creature saw them at the same time, and it stood up abruptly and stared at them.

At this point Patterson's horse began bucking and trying to turn around. Patterson grabbed the movie-camera from the saddlebag, then sprang down from the horse, which bolted off downstream. Gimlin's horse was older and more placid, but even so it began to get agitated. The Sasquatch began to walk off along the creek bank, heading for the dense forests that lined

Ape-man File

OTHER FOOTAGE

Since 1967, other footage has surfaced claiming to show the Sasquatch, though none of it matches the quality of the Patterson film. These include the Freeman footage, shot in 1994 by forestry worker Paul Freeman near Walla Walla, Washington. It shows a hairy humanlike figure crossing a path and then disappearing into woodland. The Redwoods footage (1995), filmed on a rainy night in northern California, shows a similar-looking creature moving in the beam of a car's headlights. The Manitoba footage (2005), shot on the banks of Nelson River, Manitoba, shows a strange figure on the opposite bank – but it is too distant to be sure what it is.

Scrambling back to his feet Patterson refocused the camera on the Sasquatch, which was by now walking off again. The creature turned again to look at the two men, but did not break its stride as it had done before. It continued to walk away and then passed around a bend in the canyon. That was when Patterson ran out of film, but the two men later said they could still hear the creature moving off. It seemed to be running quite fast.

Gimlin and Patterson hurriedly discussed the situation. Gimlin thought the creature had been nearly 7 ft (213 cm) tall and had weighed around 300 lb (136 kg). Patterson thought it had been 1 ft (30 cm) taller and much heavier. Both men had noticed that the creature had breasts and concluded that it was a female. Gimlin wanted to push on up the creek in pursuit of the creature, but Patterson refused. His rifle was still on his horse, which had bolted. Patterson reminded Gimlin that the tracks found by Green and Dahinden indicated that this was a family of Sasquatch, and, if the male Sasquatch was nearby, it would probably not be as timid as the female, especially if it thought they might be threatening its mate and its young.

The Footprints

After catching the two runaway horses and tying up the packhorse, they headed off upstream, taking care not to disturb the Sasquatch tracks. They followed the tracks for about 600 yd (550 m). The trail turned away from the creek and into the wooded slopes of the canyon. The tracks confirmed that the creature had headed uphill. Again, Gimlin wanted to push on, but Patterson was still nervous about the possible presence of an aggressive male.

By this time, it was late afternoon and the weather did not look too promising. Patterson wanted to go back to film and cast the footprints before night closed in. With a new film in the camera, he took extensive shots of the Sasquatch tracks and then cast the clearest footprints that he could find.

Ape-man File

WHAT DOES THE PATTERSON FILM SHOW?

Experts who have since studied the film suggest it is a female Bigfoot, as two mammary glands are just visible on its front. Some have questioned its authenticity. They say if the film is played at a slightly faster speed, it could be a human in a costume. However, aspects of the film do stand up to scientific scrutiny. For example, some biologists have said that for such a creature to walk upright, it would need an extended heel. The creature has an extended heel. Film industry experts have said that the film was not made using special effects.

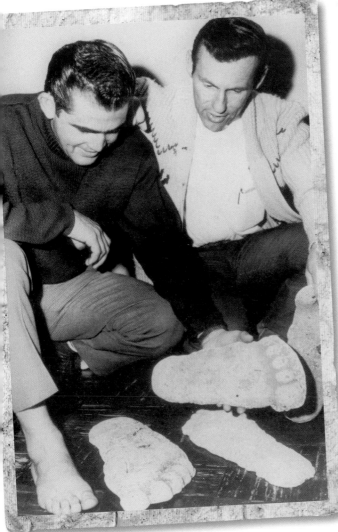

Bob Gimlin (left) and Roger Patterson compare casts of the Bigfoot prints they found.

highly excited and was worrying about how good the film would prove to be.

Studying the Tracks

Word spread quickly among Sasquatch researchers, including Bob Titmus (see pages 13–14). Titmus decided to study the tracks for himself. He arrived at the site eight days after the encounter, accompanied by his brother-in-law. Titmus took some casts of the prints that Patterson had covered over with bark and twigs. According to Titmus, they showed the Sasquatch moving exactly as Patterson and Gimlin had claimed. Starting from the creek, the creature had gone upstream and then around the canyon corner, before disappearing into the trees.

Other good prints were covered over with bark and twigs to protect them from rain.

Patterson and Gimlin rode back to their camp, then drove to the town of Eureka to send out the precious movie film for processing. On the way back to camp they stopped off at Willow Creek to see Al Hodgson and told him about the day's events. Hodgson later recalled that Patterson was

Titus also measured the stride length, confirming that it increased markedly once the Sasquatch had gone out of sight of the men. He measured the depth of the Sasquatch tracks at one point at 1.25 in (317 mm). He then measured his brother-in-law's footprints at the same point and they were 0.25 in (64 mm) deep. His brother-in-law weighed 200 lb (91 kg), so Titmus concluded that the Sasquatch must have weighed around 600 lb (272 kg).

Titmus then followed the Sasquatch tracks into the forest, well beyond the point where Patterson and Gimlin had given up the chase. He concluded that the Sasquatch had actually turned around to go back down the canyon. After a short distance, it had stopped and sat down. Looking back downhill, Titmus realized that he had an uninterrupted view of the scene of the encounter. The Sasquatch, he decided, must have sat there watching Patterson and Gimlin as they caught their horses, cast the footprints, and shot their film of the scene. It had then got up and walked off uphill and deeper into the forest.

Some months later, the site was visited by John Green. He brought with him a student by the name of Jim McClarin who, at 6 ft 5 in (198 cm), was the tallest man he could talk into accompanying him. Green stood where Patterson had been standing after his fall and filmed McClarin following the route of the Sasquatch. The movie helped determine the Sasquatch's height of around 7 ft 4 in (223 cm), and also that the creature had stepped up a 30-in (76-cm) high bank without breaking its stride.

Critical Reaction

When the film was developed, John Green arranged for it to be shown to a panel of invited scientists. Their reaction was guarded. None of them was prepared to say the film definitely showed evidence of a new species. Frank Beebe, a well-known Vancouver naturalist, said: "I'm not convinced, but I think the film is genuine. From a scientific standpoint, one of the hardest facts to go against is that there is no evidence anywhere in the continent of ape evolution."

EYEWITNESS ACCOUNT

WE NEED BONES OR A SKULL

On viewing the Patterson film, Don Abbott, an anthropologist at the Provincial Museum of British Columbia, said:

"It is about as hard to believe the film is faked as it is to admit that such a creature really lives. If there is a chance to follow up scientifically, my curiosity is such that I'd want to go along with it. Like most scientists, however, I'm not ready to put my reputation on the line until something concrete shows up – something like bones or a skull."

The film was later shown to another panel of New York scientists, who announced that in their view the film was a fake and the whole Sasquatch business was a colossal hoax. Their reasoning had nothing to do with the film itself, but rested on the grounds that it was impossible for there to be an unknown hominid ape in North America. And since that was impossible, it followed that the film had to be a fake.

Limb Proportions and Movements

Undaunted, Green and Dahinden continued to seek scientific support for the Patterson film. Dahinden contacted a British professor of biomechanics named Don Grieve. His task was to compare the limb proportions and movements of "Patty" (the nickname given to the creature in the Patterson movie) to those of a human. If Patty was a human in a hairy outfit, this would show it up. Grieve began with the limb proportions and quickly concluded that Patty had leg-to-body proportions similar to those of a man. The arms, however, were longer than those of a human and the elbow was lower down. The ratio between a human leg and arm is about 10:7; in the case of Patty, the ratio is more like 10:9.

This photograph shows the skull of a gorilla. If communities of Bigfoot are still found in the wild, why have no remains of this type yet come to light?

The Walk

One of the early objections raised to Patty's gait is that it resembles that of a man, not a woman, but the creature's breasts indicate it is clearly a female. However, Sasquatch researchers point out that walking styles are different in male and female humans because female hips are wider than those of a male. This is because the large brain of a human baby needs a large skull to accommodate it. They say that the Sasquatch does not seem any more intelligent than a gorilla, and the skull of the baby Sasquatch is therefore likely to be more like that of a baby gorilla than a baby human, so the female Sasquatch would not need to have wide hips.

Grieve studied the speed of the walk, the length of the stride, and the angles formed by the thighs and the knees as the creature moved. He concluded that the way Patty walked was very different from a normal human walk. In particular, the creature did not at any time lock its knees into a straight line, something that all humans do. This, of course, did not rule out the possibility that that the figure was a man walking in a deliberately unusual manner.

Grieve then did more calculations and came back with a query: "At what speed in frames per second (fps) had the film been shot?" The question was crucial. If the film had been shot at 24 fps or more, then a human male could have managed to mimic the walking style with a bit of effort. But if the film had been shot at a slower speed, he said, no human could have moved his legs in the manner shown. After further research (see panel), it was concluded that the actual

Ape-man File

WORKING OUT THE CAMERA SPEED

Patterson told Grieve that he usually set the movie-camera at 24 fps, but, when he had reloaded the film to shoot the tracks after the sighting, he had noticed that the camera was set to 16 fps. Perhaps it had been jolted out of its usual setting when he had stumbled, or when the camera had been bounced about in the saddlebags of his horse when it had become frightened. A Soviet researcher named Igor Bourtsev found the answer. He noted that the start of the movie showed a series of up and down shudders. It was at this point that Patterson claimed he had been running toward the Sasquatch, so Bourtsev thought that the shudders might have been caused by Patterson's feet hitting the ground. At 24 fps, the shudders indicated that Patterson had been taking 6 steps per second, but at 16 fps they indicated that he was taking four steps per second. When running it is impossible for a human to take more than five steps per second. By this means, Bourtsev calculated that the speed of the camera had been between 14 and 18 fps.

speed of the film in the camera had been between 14 and 18 fps. According to Grieve, that ruled out a man in a fur suit.

Could the Patterson film have featured a human in a costume, similar to those used in 1968's Planet of the Apes?

The Chambers Rumor

Less than 18 months after the Patterson film was shot, rumors began to filter out of the Hollywood movie industry. It was said that Patty was a man wearing a suit produced by the famous special effects and make-up artist John Chambers. Chambers had worked on a vast number of projects, including the movie *Planet of the Apes*, released in 1968. He did not confirm or deny the reports, just smiled knowingly. The story was finally laid to rest by Chambers himself in 1997 after his retirement. He gave an interview in which he denied knowing anything about Patterson, Gimlin, or their film until long after it was taken. "I was good," Chambers said, "but I was never that good."

BIGFOOT: ASSESSING THE EVIDENCE

The scientific community is united on one point. They could be convinced that the Sasquatch actually exists if someone were able to produce a living or dead specimen – or at least a significant part of one such as a skull or several bones. Before moving on to look at the evidence that *does* exist, it is worth spending a bit of time on the evidence that doesn't. Why has no one ever found a Sasquatch body?

Burying the Dead?

Cryptozoologists argue that the Sasquatch seems to be a relatively intelligent creature. It may even prove to be more intelligent than the gorilla and other large apes. It is not impossible, therefore, that the Sasquatch take steps to hide the dead bodies of family members from scavengers such as wolves or cougars. Sasquatch seekers point to archaeological evidence, which shows that respect for the dead began very early in human evolution. Neanderthal people buried their dead, and there is some evidence that burials might also have taken place among the much more primitive *Homo erectus* species.

Carnivores and Acid Soil

Another explanation offered by Sasquatch seekers focuses on the wolves, cougars, bears, and other carnivores that share the range of the Sasquatch. When a creature as big as a Sasquatch dies, the suddenly available meat would attract the attention of a large number of predators and carrion eaters. Within a matter of a days, the carcass would be picked clean. For this reason, professional hunters who spend a lot of time in wilderness areas rarely come across the dead body of a bear, an elk, or a deer.

The scavengers would, however, at least leave some bones behind, such as skulls and thigh bones, which might be expected to show up from time to time. Sasquatch seekers claim the lack of such finds can be explained by the highly acidic soil in the mountainous forests of the Pacific seaboard. The soil is usually overlaid with equally acidic coniferous leaf litter and assorted debris. Bones are highly susceptible to the leaching effects of acid. Any bone left lying on the ground would, they

Ape-man File

SHY TO THE END

Some Sasquatch researchers offer another possible explanation for the lack of bodies. They conjecture that the Sasquatch might seek shelter when it feels ill. If a sick or injured Sasquatch crawls off into dense undergrowth to be safe from cougar or wolves, and then dies, its body is less likely to be found.

argue, quickly lose calcium and other minerals and could crumble away to dust in a surprisingly short time.

Faking Footprints

The best examples of evidence for the existence of the Sasquatch are the thousands of footprints that have been found in the forests where it is said to live. But are they genuine or fake, and how can researchers tell the difference? Even the most dedicated Sasquatch believers would admit that not all the reported Sasquatch footprints are genuine. Writing in 1989, anthropologist Grover Krantz estimated that up to half of all the reported Sasquatch

footprints were probably fakes. Distinguishing between fakes and possibly genuine footprints can be difficult, but a knowledge of animal behavior can help.

When a wild animal leaves a track, it is not a simple matter of a foot being pushed down into soil, mud, or snow to leave a print. The creature is moving, and the footprints show the traces of this. Toes may dig in to get a grip when going uphill, or splay out on mud. If the creature changes direction, the foot will twist and so distort the print it leaves behind. Nor is a foot an unyielding object. It will fold around stones and other hard objects so that a footprint may well have a stone sticking up inside it.

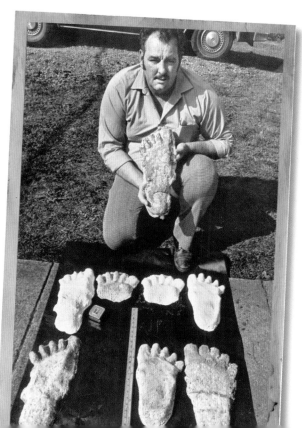

Bigfoot researcher Paul Freeman found so many prints that his colleagues became suspicious.

Most fakes are made by people using wooden plates carved to the size and shape of a Sasquatch footprint. These are then tied onto the feet and the faker walks around, leaving behind impressive-looking tracks. But the footprints left by wooden feet show no signs of movement: each print is identical to the last. Moreover, the depth of the footprint will reveal that the creator weighed too little in proportion to the size of its feet.

The famous hoaxer Ray Wallace used this method of making false Sasquatch tracks. He would strap on his wooden feet and stride on and beside trails that he knew to be heavily used by urban vacationers, who would have a limited knowledge of wild animal tracks. His efforts led to a large number of reports being made, but they were usually quickly revealed for what they were once an experienced researcher got to see them first hand.

These fake prints were made by Ray Wallace, using a pair of hand-carved wooden feet.

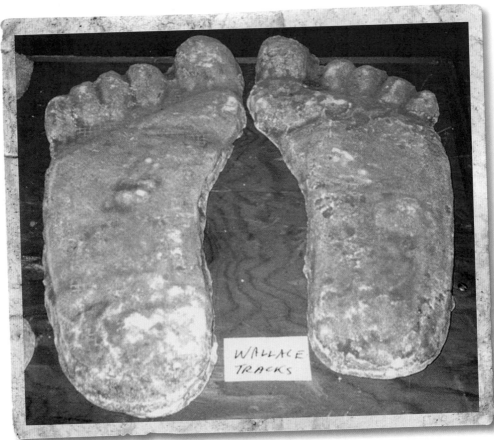

WALLACE TRACKS

Rubber Feet

A more sophisticated method of faking Bigfoot tracks emerged in the later 1980s. A number of tracks and footprints began to be found that, although obviously not created by wooden feet, were suspect. They had been made by a soft, foot-like object, but while they showed some signs of dynamic interaction between the foot and the ground, they did not show the foot or the toes moving or flexing in any way.

Researchers were suspicious, but puzzled. It was Donald Baird, of the Carnegie Museum of Natural History, who worked out how they had probably been produced. Baird was a palaeontologist who specialized in latex and rubber molds. He showed how the fake feet could have been created using silicone rubber and cheesecloth. They were then tamped down into the earth with a hammer. Such a method can create surprisingly realistic prints, but even so it cannot mimic a muscled foot that changes its shape or grip during a step, nor is it much good on softer ground. Once researchers knew how the fake prints could be created, they could spot the frauds more easily.

Built for Grip

The press gave Sasquatch the name "Bigfoot" because the footprints discovered by Jerry Crew were so large.

Ape-man File

CLEVER HOAX

In January 1991, a Sasquatch footprint trail was reported near Mill Creek, Washington. It was investigated by researcher James Hewkin. At first sight, the footprints seemed genuine enough, but the route of the track raised suspicions. The track began high on a snow-covered hill, ran down through woods to cross a field where winter wheat was starting to sprout, crossed a road, headed for a stream, then cut back to the road where the footprints ended. The fact that the trail ended at a road was suspicious in itself. Moreover, for much of their length the footprints showed a clear tendency for the feet to be splayed – a human characteristic. Where the tracks crossed a fence, the prints were set exactly where a biped of human height would put them, though the size of the prints indicated that they had been made by a Sasquatch over 7 ft (213 cm) tall. One footprint was curiously deformed and slashed. Careful analysis showed that the mark had been made by the "foot" toppling sideways and leaving a flat depression. The conclusion was that the "feet" were rubber or silicone fakes that had been mounted on flat-sided blocks, probably of wood, and then strapped onto the feet of a human.

Most of the Sasquatch footprints that have been discovered since that time have also been large: lengths of 15 in (37 cm) and widths of 6 in (15 cm) are not unusual.

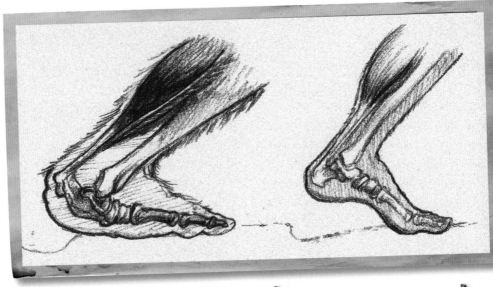

But size is not the only distinguishing feature. According to researchers, Sasquatch footprints are a different shape to those of humans, and show signs of differences in foot structure as well. The foot of a Sasquatch, cryptid researchers say, is wider in proportion to its length than the human foot. Its heel and toes are more elongated. They deduce from the prints that the toes are long and strongly muscled. In addition, Sasquatch feet usually leave an impression that is flat across the whole sole because, unlike the human foot, there is no arch. Researchers also claim that Sasquatch feet are more flexible. They often show a "midtarsal break," indicated by a clear ridging of the soil or mud about halfway along the footprint. It is caused by the foot bending at this point as the weight of the animal is transferred to the front of the foot. Human footprints do not show

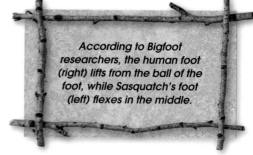

According to Bigfoot researchers, the human foot (right) lifts from the ball of the foot, while Sasquatch's foot (left) flexes in the middle.

this feature because the human foot cannot bend at this point (near the ankle): the midtarsal bones are fused solid. The flexibility of the Sasquatch foot, as well as its long, muscular toes, suggests to researchers that the Sasquatch foot has good gripping ability, useful for negotiating the steep slopes of its mountainous habitat.

The Skookum Cast

One of the most impressive tracks allegedly left by a Sasquatch is the so-called Skookum Cast. The story began in September 2000, when the

Bigfoot Field Researchers Organization (BFRO) organized a ten-man expedition into the Skookum Meadows area of Washington State to look for footprints and other signs of Sasquatch. Using loudspeakers, they played a recording of a call thought to have been made by a Sasquatch, in the hope that it would provoke a response. The team also put out baits of fruit on sites next to soft soil. It was hoped that a Sasquatch might be attracted by the fruit and, in collecting it, leave tracks behind.

On September 22, two of the team went out to inspect the fruit baits. One of the baits had been taken. The fruit had been picked up and most of it had been eaten. A few pieces of debris showed the marks of broad, flat teeth. What at first puzzled the researchers was that there were no footprints in the muddy ground where the fruit had been placed. Then they spotted an odd series of marks in the soft soil. It looked as though some large animal had lain down there.

Other members of the team were called in to look at the impression. One of them noticed what seemed to be a heel imprint. Another saw what looked like an arm imprint. The team concluded that a Sasquatch had seen the fruit, but had decided not to walk into the mud to get it. Instead it had lain down next to the mud and then reached out with its arm to grab it.

It was decided to cast the impression in plaster. The cast measured 5 ft (152 cm) by 3 ft (91 cm) and was carefully shipped out to Seattle, where a team of scientists was called together. The team included anthropologists Grover Krantz (see page 29) and Jeff Meldrum, wildlife biologist Dr. John Bindernagle, and African game specialist Dr. Ron Brown. They carefully cleaned up the cast by removing soil that had stuck to it. Any hair caught in the plaster was bagged up for analysis. Most of the hair would turn out to belong to elk, deer, and bear, but there were also numerous strands that could not be identified.

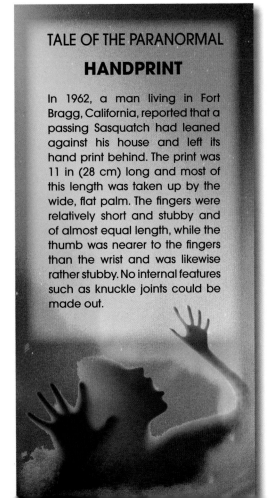

TALE OF THE PARANORMAL

HANDPRINT

In 1962, a man living in Fort Bragg, California, reported that a passing Sasquatch had leaned against his house and left its hand print behind. The print was 11 in (28 cm) long and most of this length was taken up by the wide, flat palm. The fingers were relatively short and stubby and of almost equal length, while the thumb was nearer to the fingers than the wrist and was likewise rather stubby. No internal features such as knuckle joints could be made out.

The cast itself showed that a large creature had lain down and left its body impression. It seemed to be the impression of a large human-shaped creature resting on its left side. The marks of the left forearm, left leg, left buttock, and left side of the body were quite clear. The only sign of the right leg was the heel, which had been pushed deep into the soft ground as if to steady the creature. The cast also showed clear marks of hair striations, indicating that the thing that had lain down was covered by thick hair.

The scientific team sent out a press release. The wording was suitably cautious, stating only that the cast "constitutes compelling and significant new evidence" but stopping short of claiming that it had been produced by a Sasquatch. Skeptics responded that the Skookum Cast was most likely caused by an elk lying down.

Sasquatch "Nests"

When he returned from his alleged kidnapping by a family of Sasquatch, Albert Ostman (see pages 6–11) mentioned that the creatures had slept on what he called "blankets" made out of woven fir branches and moss.

On May 13, 2001, researcher Kathy Moskowitz came across three structures

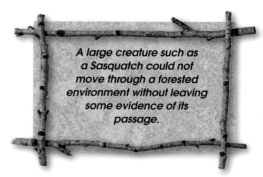

A large creature such as a Sasquatch could not move through a forested environment without leaving some evidence of its passage.

in the forests near Sonora, California, that seemed to have been deliberately constructed. They were each built out of natural materials that could have been gathered nearby. Since Sasquatch had been reported in the vicinity, she suspected that they might be nests or sleeping areas. The largest and most complete of the nests was unusual in that it had a roof formed out of a 12-ft (3.5-m) tall oak sapling that had been bent over and held down with a large rock. A number of pine branches were then leaned against or pushed into the branches of the sapling to form a solid wall of vegetation that would have effectively kept out wind or rain. The sheltered floor of the nest was padded with leaves, ferns, moss, and other vegetation.

Other researchers have found similar structures, as well as piles of pine branches or ferns that might be nests. Most of these structures were found in wooded areas and lay on the ground with no attempt at overhead cover. One apparent nest was found in 1988 inside an abandoned mine entrance. It measured 4 ft (122 cm) by 4 ft 6 in (137 cm). The base was made of piled sticks that had been covered over with a layer of dead leaves. On top of this was a thick layer of fresh leaves, moss, ferns, and other vegetation.

There is no direct evidence that these nests were built or used by Sasquatch.

Nobody has reported seeing a Sasquatch sleeping in one, nor have tracks been followed that lead to a nest. However, the construction of the nests would require hands to manipulate the branches and other components. The only possible candidates for the builders of these nests are Sasquatch or humans.

Ape-man File

SNOW MOUNDS

In 2007, researchers became aware of another type of structure that might be constructed by Sasquatch. Snow mounds take the form of a mound of snow about 3–4 ft (91–122 cm) high and up to 12 ft (3.5 m) across. Once the mound has been created and its surface smoothed over, it is covered by a thick layer of wood chips, bark, branches, and other woody debris. The woody material is usually arranged so that it entirely covers, and so insulates, the snow. When the snow covering the ground melts away, the snow mound remains intact, taking several days to melt away. When snow mounds have been dug into, they have been found to contain nothing but snow. What these structures are for and whether they are even related to the Sasquatch enigma are hotly debated topics. The sites on which the snow mounds have been found have generally been far from human habitation or activity. Are they built to keep stored food cold? Like so much to do with the Sasquatch, they are a mystery.

THE SKUNK APE

Reports of a mysterious wild ape from the southeastern United States have attracted much less publicity than the Bigfoot phenomenon of the northwestern states. Sasquatch researchers are divided in their reactions. Some treat the reports of the southeastern ape as if it were part of the same Sasquatch enigma. Others tend to ignore them because they do not fit the pattern for the Sasquatch of the forested mountains of the Pacific northwest. Still others, however, see them as evidence of something different from the Sasquatch. The southeastern creature has been called the Skunk Ape because of the terrible smell that is so often associated with its alleged appearances. The majority of the reports have come from Florida, so the creature is also sometimes called the Florida Ape.

Early Reports

The earliest reported sighting came in 1900. The local newspaper in Hannibal, Missouri, reported that a strange ape creature had been seen on an island in the Mississippi. It had been captured by a passing circus, which claimed that it was their escaped orangutan. They had not, however, reported a missing animal, and orangutans cannot swim, which makes its appearance on the island something of a puzzle. A second report comes from 1949. Two fishermen out on Sugar Creek, Indiana, were allegedly chased off by a rather aggressive creature that they identified as a "gorilla." However, it was not until the 1960s that reports began to be made in any real numbers.

One of the first of these came from Davis, West Virginia, in 1960. A group of young men were camping out in some woods. One of them felt a sudden dig in his ribs. Thinking it was a friend wanting his attention, he turned around. Instead, according to the witness, he found himself looking at a 8-ft (244-cm) tall figure covered in long, shaggy hair. The creature, he later said, had enormous eyes that glowed as if with some sort of inner fire. After frightening the teenager, the beast allegedly walked off into the trees.

This photograph allegedly shows a Florida Skunk Ape.

Another reported sighting came from Clanton, Alabama, in the same year. The Reverend E.C. Hand and half a dozen others claimed they saw an ape of some sort bounding along beside Route 31. They called Sheriff T.J. Lockhart, who went to investigate. He found two sets of tracks, one larger than the other. The larger footprints were about the size of a man's foot, with the big toe sticking out sideways, while the smaller footprints were identical in shape, but half the size.

Ape-man File

SIMIAN SIMILARITIES

Based on the reports of sightings, the Skunk Ape would seem to be quite a different creature from the Sasquatch of the Pacific northwest. The Sasquatch is routinely described as being a massive creature walking upright like a human. In comparison, the Skunk Ape is usually reported as being smaller, and it either walks on all fours or with a waddling gait if upright. It is generally described as being very like a chimpanzee or an orangutan.

The hind feet of chimpanzees, orangutans, and gorillas all have a big toe that sticks out sideways, more like a thumb. This is because they use their hind legs for grasping as well as for walking. Nor do they habitually walk on their hind feet, but rather on all fours. When they do this, they curl their hands into loose fists and support themselves on their knuckles. This way of moving demands a particular kind of bone structure in the hind foot, one that allows the big toe to remain prehensile. The apes being seen in the damp or swampy forest lands of the southeastern states of the United States were, it appears, apes of this kind.

Glowing Eyes

On the evening of November 30, 1966, a woman got a flat tire while driving along a rural road near Brooksville, Florida. She got out to change the tire and was halfway through the process when she saw something moving in the trees. Worried that it might be somebody up to no good, she looked more closely and – according to her later testimony – saw an apelike figure covered in hair. As it got closer, she said, the figure's eyes seemed to glow a weird greenish color as they reflected the light from her flashlight. She got back into her car and waited for a passing vehicle that she could flag down.

Like an Orangutan

A pair of workmen reported a strange experience in May 1973. They were working on some vacation houses in the Florida Everglades, near Naples. On the second day, at around dusk, one of the men heard something moving about in the swampy forest nearby. According to the workman, he looked up to see a pair of eyes glaring at him

According to witnesses, the Skunk Ape looks similar to an orangutan.

from the undergrowth, about 20 ft (6 m) away. At first he thought it was a bear, but when it moved he saw that the face was more like that of a human. Around it were strands of long, wispy hair. Concerned for his safety, the man began to back off. When he felt that it was safe to do so, he ran to one of the vacation houses where the men had some guns. The men watched from the windows as the creature came out of the trees. It walked, they said, on its hind legs, but with an odd, waddling gait. Then it grabbed some of the food that they had been preparing to cook on a camp fire, before slipping back into the trees. In hindsight, the main witness thought that the creature was closest in look to an orangutan. When the men emerged from the house, they noticed a strong smell that one of them likened to a pigsty that needed to be cleaned.

Seen from a Car

Many reported sightings of Skunk Apes have been by motorists driving through rural areas. For instance, a woman was driving back to her rural home in December 1985 after completing her night shift at work. Driving along the highway from Tavares, she allegedly saw a large animal move out of the woods. The creature, she later said, was walking on its hind legs, but she did not get a good look at it. She slowed down as she passed the place where it had entered the trees and rolled down the car window to get a better look. Although she could not see anything, she said she was hit by a deeply offensive stench.

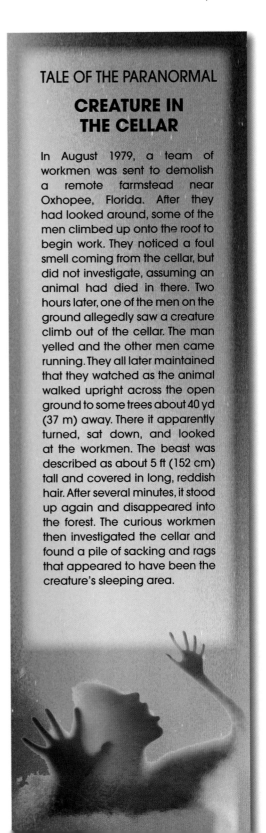

TALE OF THE PARANORMAL

CREATURE IN THE CELLAR

In August 1979, a team of workmen was sent to demolish a remote farmstead near Oxhopee, Florida. After they had looked around, some of the men climbed up onto the roof to begin work. They noticed a foul smell coming from the cellar, but did not investigate, assuming an animal had died in there. Two hours later, one of the men on the ground allegedly saw a creature climb out of the cellar. The man yelled and the other men came running. They all later maintained that they watched as the animal walked upright across the open ground to some trees about 40 yd (37 m) away. There it apparently turned, sat down, and looked at the workmen. The beast was described as about 5 ft (152 cm) tall and covered in long, reddish hair. After several minutes, it stood up again and disappeared into the forest. The curious workmen then investigated the cellar and found a pile of sacking and rags that appeared to have been the creature's sleeping area.

Another road-related sighting came in August 2004, when Jennifer Ward was driving through Polk County, Florida. It was evening, and her two young daughters were asleep in the back of her vehicle. As she passed near Green Swamp, she saw what she took to be a human bending down in a roadside ditch. She slowed down to ask if she could offer any help. As she was getting out of the car, the figure stood up. Ward said later that she was shocked to find herself confronted by a hairy, apelike figure about 8 ft (244 cm) tall. Putting the safety of her daughters ahead of any curiosity, Ward sped off.

Close to Green Cove Spring, Florida, in 1986, a mother and her son claimed to have a similar experience when they were driving along State Route 209 late one evening. Suddenly, a humanlike figure, about 5 ft (152 cm) tall and covered all over in hair, allegedly appeared in the headlights. It glanced quickly at the approaching vehicle and then bounded off the road to slip away among the trees.

Another encounter took place on Turner Road outside Everglades City in 2001. This time the creature was reportedly squatting by the side of the road. It was about 3 ft (91 cm) tall when in a sitting position. The driver slowed down to get a closer look, but, as the car approached, the animal apparently got up onto all fours. Its front legs were described as much longer than its back legs and it was covered in brown hair. It then

This artist's impression shows Jennifer Ward's encounter with a Skunk Ape.

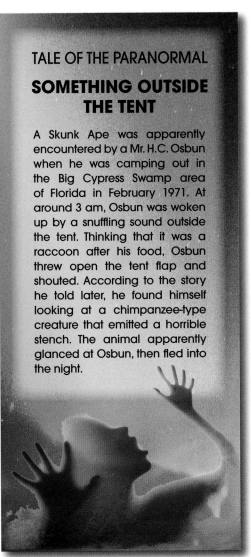

SOMETHING OUTSIDE THE TENT

A Skunk Ape was apparently encountered by a Mr. H.C. Osbun when he was camping out in the Big Cypress Swamp area of Florida in February 1971. At around 3 am, Osbun was woken up by a snuffling sound outside the tent. Thinking that it was a raccoon after his food, Osbun threw open the tent flap and shouted. According to the story he told later, he found himself looking at a chimpanzee-type creature that emitted a horrible stench. The animal apparently glanced at Osbun, then fled into the night.

moved off quickly and disappeared into some trees. The driver thought that it looked like a chimpanzee.

Anonymous Letter

On December 29, 2000, the Sheriff's Office in Sarasota, Florida, received a letter addressed to the "Animal Services Department." The letter was from a lady asking if any local zoo or circus had lost an orangutan, since one had been visiting her property recently. Enclosed with the letter were two photographs of the said ape. The sheriff knew of no exotic animals that had been reported lost. On January 3, he contacted David Barkasy of the nearby Silver City Serpentarium for advice. Barkasy, who knew about the local legend, wondered if the photographs were actually of the Skunk Ape.

Unfortunately the letter was anonymous. All the writer said was that she and her husband were retired and were living near the Myakka State Park. In February, the pictures and some comments from the letter were released to the local press and media in the hope that the writer of the letter could be persuaded to come forward. To date, she has not done so.

The photographs were sent to Loren Coleman, a noted Bigfoot researcher, who analyzed them himself before sending copies to assorted photographic and primate experts. All came to the conclusion that the photographs had not been produced by digital tampering or other fraudulent means. The creature that was depicted seems to be very similar to an orangutan. Even its facial expression is similar to that of an orangutan that is showing fear or surprise, which would be natural if its evening foraging were suddenly interrupted by a camera flash.

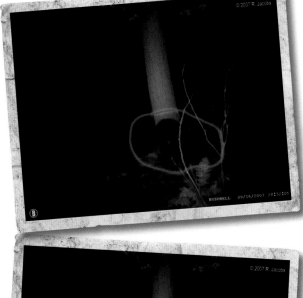

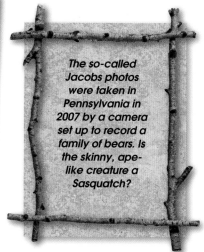

Violent Behaviour

The Sasquatch of the northwestern United States is typically described as a placid, shy creature that would sooner avoid encounters with humans. Occasionally, however, reports come in of a more violent kind of creature. These have mostly come from the eastern USA. Among the more famous of these reports was a string of cases from around Fouke in Kentucky. They told of a Bigfoot-type creature that behaved in an aggressive, often terrifying way toward humans. Typical of these was the Ford case.

On the night of May 1, 1971, Mrs. Ford was woken up by the sound of her bedroom window opening. Through the open window, so she later claimed, came a hairy arm bearing a large, clawed hand that grasped out for her. Behind the

The so-called Jacobs photos were taken in Pennsylvania in 2007 by a camera set up to record a family of bears. Is the skinny, ape-like creature a Sasquatch?

window, Mrs. Ford said she glimpsed an apelike face. When she screamed, the arm and the face retreated. Mr. Ford grabbed a gun and ran out of the house. He said he arrived just in time to see a Sasquatch figure. He fired, but the creature apparently slipped off into the trees unharmed. An hour later, the couple reported, the beast came back, on this occasion trying to kick the front door down. Ford shot at it again, and this time it left for good.

Joan Mills and Mary Ryan stopped for a picnic near the town of Louisiana, Missouri, in July 1971. They had just laid out their meal when – so they later reported – a Bigfoot came lumbering out of some nearby bushes. It was making what they described as a weird gurgling noise and was behaving in a threatening manner. The two women fled to their car and locked themselves in, but they could not drive away because they had left the keys with their picnic. Then, according to their report, the Bigfoot lumbered up to the car and tried to open the doors. Unable to do so, it turned to the picnic and ate some food before returning to the undergrowth from which it had emerged. Once it was gone, Mills retrieved the keys, and they drove off.

In the same month, a Bigfoot allegedly visited a farm near Shapsville, Indiana, on five separate occasions. Each time, according to the farmer, it came at night, and once it attacked the farm dog, though without inflicting serious injury. The farmer said he shot at it several times, but never seemed able to hit the thing.

A couple of years later, in June 1973, four teenage girls were in a car sheltering from a thunderstorm when they were allegedly approached by a 8-ft (244-cm) tall Bigfoot that growled and screamed at them. The beast, they said, had large eyes that glowed bright red. Although the teenagers drove off at high speed, the Bigfoot seemed able to move even quicker because they apparently saw it standing beside the road ahead of them as they sped off. When they reached the home of one of the girls, the Bigfoot was waiting – so they say. After glaring at them with its red eyes, it walked off.

Ape-man File

THE EASTERN BIGFOOT

A few cryptozoologists have suggested that there might be a subspecies or variant of the Sasquatch, which they call the Eastern Bigfoot. It is suggested that this Eastern Bigfoot has developed a more aggressive streak and more threatening behavior because it lives in closer proximity to humans. If so, the Eastern Bigfoot would be an unusual creature. The usual reaction of large mammals faced by a growing human population is to move away or to become more retiring.

THE YETI

The Yeti – or "Abominable Snowman," as the press called it – hit the news headlines in the year 1951. British mountaineer Eric Shipton returned from an expedition to the Himalayas with some photographs taken in the high mountain snows. They were of a series of footprints that ran for hundreds of yards across a snowfield. Although the footprints were roughly human in outline, they were enormous. The photographs dominated the British newspapers for days and the story rapidly spread to other countries.

The purpose of Shipton's Himalayan trip had been to discover routes up the lower sections of the Everest massif in readiness for a later attempt on the peak itself. Shipton and his colleague Michael Ward were exploring the saddle at the top of the Menlung Glacier at around 18,000 ft (5,486 m) when they saw a set of tracks left in deep snow. They followed them for about a mile (1,600 m) along the edge of the glacier, but then had to turn back. In order to prove their story, they photographed a section of the track and one of the clearest individual prints.

Early Encounters

Even if the general public was surprised by these pictures, mountaineers and travellers in the Himalayas were less shocked. For decades, they had been hearing stories about the strange half-human, half-ape beasts that lurked in the

This photograph sparked international interest in the Yeti.

mountains. The only surprise was that somebody had finally managed to photograph a series of tracks.

The first outsider to hear tales of the strange beasts was the hill walker B.H. Hodgson. He was in northern Nepal in 1825 when his porters reported seeing a tall creature covered with long, dark hair, which bounded off in apparent fear. Hodgson did not see the creature himself, but, from the descriptions given by his excited porters, he thought that it must have been some sort of orangutan.

In 1889, Major L.A. Waddell was on a mapping expedition in the mountains of Sikkim when he found a trackway of footprints that seemed to be those of a barefooted man with enormous feet. His guide declared that they belonged to "the hairy wild man" and insisted that they should leave the area at once.

In 1925, Narik Tombazi, a Fellow of the Royal Geographical Society, reported an encounter with the Abominable Snowman. He was studying glaciers in northern Sikkim when he claims he saw a strange figure moving slowly along a path about 2,000 feet (610 m) below him. The creature was walking upright like a human, but it was covered in dense fur. It stopped every now and then to pluck leaves from bushes and once to uproot a bush and gnaw on its roots.

TALE OF THE PARANORMAL

A WARNING CRY

In 1899, Mary MacDonald, the daughter of a colonial officer, was walking through the mountains close to the border with Tibet. She was on a month-long hiking trip and had a team of porters to carry her tent, cooking equipment, and supplies. As the column was about to enter a narrow gorge on the way to the Garbyang Pass, the rocks echoed to a strange call. MacDonald later likened it to the call of a seagull, but very much louder, ending in a throaty roar. Puzzled, MacDonald turned around to ask her guide what animal could make such a noise. She found herself alone. Her guide and porters had thrown down their loads and were running away at high speed back down the track.

Now rather worried, MacDonald retrieved her hunting rifle from one of the abandoned packs, in case the unknown animal turned out to be dangerous, and set off after her porters. She found them grouped on a flat area of ground some 2 miles (3.2 km) from the gorge. They told her that the cry had been made by a *metoh kangmi*, or "bad man of the snow," which was warning them to leave. It was only after much persuasion and some threats that MacDonald got her men to retrieve the abandoned packs, but nothing would persuade them to enter the gorge.

Figures on a Mountainside

In September 1921, Colonel Howard-Bury was near Lhapka-la on his way to scout out Mount Everest for a climbing expedition. Suddenly his porters started chattering excitedly to each other and then began pointing to the side of a mountain half a mile (800 m) or so ahead. Howard-Bury looked for the source of their interest and saw – so he later alleged – three humanlike figures walking across a large patch of snow. Some hours later the expedition reached the snowfield, and he was able to study the tracks left by the figures. Each footprint, he later reported, was over 14 in (40 cm) long, but otherwise looked like that of a naked human foot. The porters told Howard-Bury that the figures were not men but *metoh kangmi*.

Ape-man File

WHAT'S IN A NAME?

Colonel Howard-Bury translated the phrase *metoh kangmi* as "Abominable Snowman." He passed on the story to a Calcutta-based journalist named Henry Newman, who wrote a few pieces about the mystery animal, again calling it the Abominable Snowman. This was the name that was used when tales of the mystery creature first spread through the English-speaking communities of northern India.

In the postwar period the name "Yeti" began to be applied to the creature. The word is not, in fact, very accurate, being derived from *yeh-the*, a generic Nepalese term for any large animal that lives in the high mountains. This has led to some confusion over the years. Locals may refer to the Himalayan red bear as a *yeh-the*, since it is large and lives in the high mountains. Many later travellers who heard stories about the aggressive Yeti had in fact been listening to tales of encounters with the red bear.

The 1954 Expedition

In 1954, the British *Daily Mail* financed an expedition to the Himalayas. The aim was to collect information about the Yeti – and catch one, if possible. The expedition organizers hired 300 porters to carry the equipment up into the high mountains, where hundreds of locals were contacted and vast distances were covered. No Yeti was captured, nor even seen, but the expedition did come back with a wealth of anecdotal evidence and a great boost in sales for the newspaper.

Among the more exciting discoveries of the expedition was the fact that two Yeti scalps were allegedly kept in Buddhist monasteries at Pangboche and Khumjung. They were used in temple rituals and dances by monks who pretended to be Yetis. The *Daily Mail* team was allowed to photograph the Pangboche scalp, but they could not borrow it for study. In 1960, the mountaineer Sir Edmund Hillary was allowed to borrow the Khumjung scalp in return for having the monastic school rebuilt. Tests revealed that the skin had come from the hide of a serow, a form of wild Himalayan goat.

The Yeti Hand

The Pangboche monastery also claimed to have a mummified Yeti hand. The monastic officials were reluctant to allow Europeans to see the relic, with good reason, as it turned out. In 1959, an American team was given permission to view and photograph it. A team member named Peter Byrne reportedly stole a few bones from the wrist and replaced them with human bones. Byrne claimed that he handed the bones to the actor James Stewart, who smuggled them back to the United States for him. When the bones were later studied, they turned out to be almost identical to those of a human, but rather larger and more robust than normal.

Meanwhile, the Pangboche Hand was studied by Sir Edmund Hillary, who decided that it was a fake made up of animal and human remains mixed

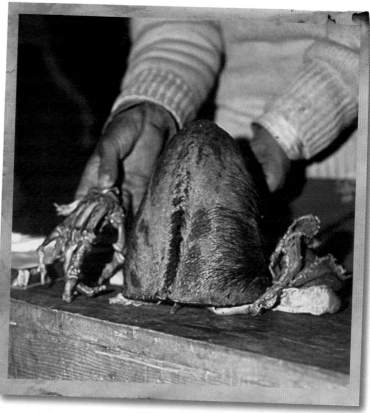

This scalp and hand, alleged to have belonged to a Yeti, were kept for many years at the remote Pangboche Monastery.

together. If Byrne did steal some bones and replace them with human bones, this might explain Hillary's findings. In 1992, the hand was stolen from the Pangboche monastery. It has not been seen since and is thought to have vanished into the illegal trade in rare animal artifacts.

Unexpected Appearances

The Yeti seems to have a habit of appearing when least expected, as it allegedly did in the following instances. In 1970, Don Whillans was camping on an open slope at 13,000 ft (3,962 m). It was shortly after dusk on a sparklingly clear moonlit night and he was resting quietly when he saw something emerge from a patch of nearby woodland. He saw the creature distinctly, and he estimated it to be about as tall as a human, but much bulkier. The beast went bounding across the turf on all fours, moving in a similar manner to a chimpanzee.

Two years later, a zoological expedition was camped out in the forested Arun Valley when a large creature came lumbering between the tents after dark. Assuming it to be a bear, the team members stayed in their tents until the creature had gone. When they emerged, they found that their visitor had left tracks that looked similar to those of a gorilla.

Then, in 1984, mountaineer David Sheppard was near the southern col of Everest when he allegedly saw a large, hairy man-like creature following him for a while. The sightings by Whillans and Sheppard are the only occasions on which credible European witnesses have seen a Yeti when visibility has been good. There have, however, been numerous sightings by Sherpas and other hill peoples, who spend far more time in the Himalayas than Europeans.

Sightings by Sherpas

In March 1951, Lakhpa Tensing went up to the hill pastures above Namche to search for a missing yak. There, according to his later account, he came across a 5-ft (152-cm) tall Yeti squatting on a rock and eating a mousehare. The Yeti, he reported, quickly scampered off. A few years later, Pasang Nima was leading a caravan over the Nepalese–Tibet border when

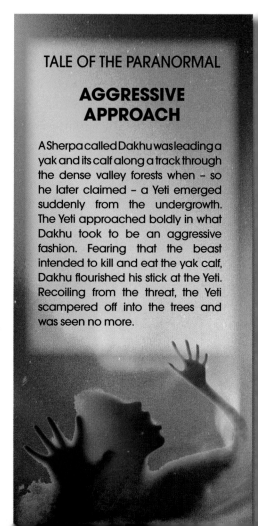

TALE OF THE PARANORMAL

AGGRESSIVE APPROACH

A Sherpa called Dakhu was leading a yak and its calf along a track through the dense valley forests when – so he later claimed – a Yeti emerged suddenly from the undergrowth. The Yeti approached boldly in what Dakhu took to be an aggressive fashion. Fearing that the beast intended to kill and eat the yak calf, Dakhu flourished his stick at the Yeti. Recoiling from the threat, the Yeti scampered off into the trees and was seen no more.

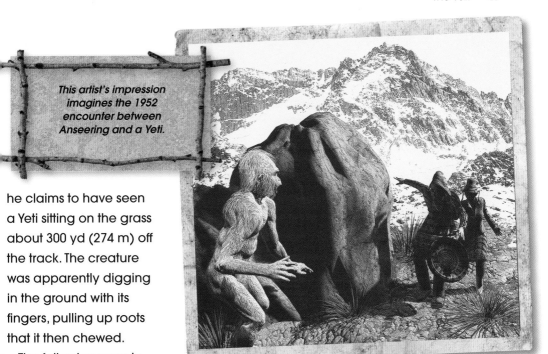

This artist's impression imagines the 1952 encounter between Anseering and a Yeti.

he claims to have seen a Yeti sitting on the grass about 300 yd (274 m) off the track. The creature was apparently digging in the ground with its fingers, pulling up roots that it then chewed.

The following year, in October, Anseering and his wife went up to the high pastures to look for medicinal roots. According to their later report, they emerged from some trees to see a Yeti apparently picking leaves off a bush. As soon as it became aware of them, it bounded off on all four legs at high speed to disappear among a jumble of rocks.

Chinese Yeti

In the 1970s, reports of a creature very similar to the Yeti began to filter out of China. It was said to live on the Chinese side of the Himalayas, in Yunan province. The first of these was a retelling of a news item from 1962. Apparently, soldiers patrolling the passes between China and Tibet got hungry and shot a creature that, from the description they later gave of it, was some large, unknown type of ape. They ate the flesh and threw away the bones, so there was no solid evidence to back up the story.

Another report came from 1976 and told of how six forestry workers came across a strange tailless animal covered in red-brown fur. The description seemed to be that of an ape. This report prompted the Chinese Academy of Sciences to send a team to investigate the matter. They produced a number of eyewitness reports, plus a few strands of hair collected from the bark of a tree against which one of the mystery animals had been seen to lean. The hairs could not be identified.

EYEWITNESS ACCOUNT

HAIRY MAN

Pang Gensheng, a 33-year-old farmer from Cuifeng, China, describes an alleged encounter with a Yeti:

"In the summer of 1977, I went to Dadi Valley to cut logs. Between 11 am and noon, I ran into the 'hairy man' in the woods. It came closer and I got scared, so I retreated until my back was against a stone cliff and I could not go any further. The creature came up to about 5 feet (152 cm) from me. I raised my axe, ready to fight for my life. We stood like that, neither of us moving for a long time. Then I groped for a stone and threw it at him. It hit his chest. He uttered several howls and rubbed the spot with his left hand. Then he turned left and leaned against a tree, then walked away slowly toward the bottom of the valley. He kept making a mumbling sound."

Forming a Picture

The picture that emerges from these assorted descriptions from alleged witnesses is that – if it exists at all – the Yeti is an apelike creature about 5 ft (152 cm) tall on its hind feet. It moves habitually on all fours, but can walk upright for short distances. The creature seems to be mostly nocturnal, although it will occasionally come out in daylight. It seems to be omnivorous, feeding on plants and small animals when it can catch them. Most sightings of the Yeti or its footprints are of a solitary animal. It has been speculated that these may be young males driven out of the family group to find a new territory, which would explain why they are seen at all. A creature in unfamiliar territory is more likely to be spotted than one on its home ground. It also seems to be the case that the usual home of these creatures is not in the high, snowy mountains, but in the densely forested valleys where it would be most likely to find food.

Enlarged Tracks?

However, the existence of an unknown ape species is not the only explanation for some of the evidence. Could the footprints in the snow be misleading? When exposed to bright sunlight, crisp snow can evaporate straight to water vapor without first forming meltwater. When this happens, any marks in the snow can become enlarged without there being any obvious signs of melting. It is possible that some of the huge footprints that have been discovered on the high snows have become enlarged in this way.

The prime suspects for leaving such tracks are the *sadhus*, or holy men, who make a habit of living in the most remote places and in the most austere conditions. Some are said to have mastered the practice of tumo: controlling their body temperature at will by the power of their minds, allowing them to withstand the harshest winter weather. Another possible suspect is a very rare subspecies of the Asiatic brown bear, usually called the Himalayan Bear. It is known to be more likely to walk upright on its hind legs than other types of bear.

Could the Yeti Be an Ape?

Many Yeti seekers hold fast to the belief that the creature is some unrecognized species of ape. They speculate that a small population of a species previously thought extinct might have survived in the remote forests of the Himalayas. The fossil record for apes, particularly those in Asia, is sparse, but the few remains that have turned up show that apes were once far more widely distributed across southern Asia than they are today.

One of these was the massive *Gigantopithecus*, which apparently became extinct around 150,000 years ago. This ape lived across India, Southeast Asia, and southern China. Fossils of the ape reveal it was a massive 9 ft (273 cm) tall on its hind legs. Could the Yeti, if it exists, be descended from *Gigantopithecus* or some other ape species long thought dead? We simply don't know.

Could the Yeti be an ape that has adapted to cold climates? If so, it might look similar to this albino gorilla.

THE MARICOXI

In recent years the word "Maricoxi" has become a generic term for any of the cryptid primates that are rumored to live in the tropical rainforests of South America. These go by such names as Aluxes, Goazis, Aigypans, Vasitris, Matuyus, Curupiras, Curinqueans, Didi, Mono Grande, and Mapinguary. Whether or not each name indicates a different cryptid is unclear. Some or all of the names might refer to the same creature.

Hairy Hominids

The Maricoxi themselves are, or were, supposedly an extremely primitive tribe of hominids living in the Mato Grosso, a vast upland region of southern Brazil and northern Paraguay made up of forest and dense scrub. The Maricoxi were allegedly discovered by the English explorer Percy Fawcett in 1914. According to his description of the encounter with the ferocious tribe, he barely escaped with his life. He described the Maricoxi as apelike people, completely covered in hair, who spoke in grunts. Yet they lived in villages and used bows and arrows.

According to Bigfoot believers, the rainforests of South America could be home to several different species of ape-men.

MAN OF THE WOODS

The first outsider to record stories of hair-covered humans was the German naturalist Alexander von Humboldt, who mapped much of the Orinoco River in the early 1800s. He wrote:

"On the Orinoco, it is rumored the existence of a hairy man of the woods called Salvaje, that carries off women, constructs huts, and sometimes eats human flesh. The Tamanacs call him Achi, and the Maypures named him Vasitri or 'great devil.' The natives and the missionaries have no doubt of the existence of this man-shaped monkey, of which they entertain a singular dread. Father Gili (a local missionary) gravely relates the history of a lady in the town of San Carlos, in the Llanos of Venezuela, who much praised the gentle character and attentions of the man of the woods. She is stated to have lived several years with one in great domestic harmony, and only requested some hunters to take her back, 'because she and her children (a little hairy also) were weary of living far from the church and the sacraments.'"

The Mono Grande and the Didi

Another cryptid ape-man of South America is the Mono Grande, which translates as "giant monkey." As its name suggests, this hair-covered beast is usually described as standing about 5 ft (152 cm) tall. It allegedly reacts badly to humans, thrashing branches, screaming aggressively, and charging at intruders. These seem to be mere displays, however, because very few people have reported being injured by a Mono Grande.

A similar legendary creature goes by the name of the Didi. The creature is very similar to the Mono Grande. Both live in the dense rainforests of northern South America. They are also about the same size and have similar habits. The only difference seems to be that the Mono Grande has a short tail, while the Didi has none. However, some researchers believe that the two cryptids are in fact the same animal.

A book written in 1553 by the Spanish explorer Pedro de Cieza de León features the first written report of a Mono Grande. He mentioned that the local tribesmen told him about this creature, but that he never saw one himself.

The naturalist Edward Bancroft wrote in his *An Essay on the Natural History of Guiana* (1769): "It is much larger than either the African ape (chimpanzee) or the Oriental ape (orangutan), if the accounts of the natives may be relied upon. They are represented by the Indians as being near 5 feet (152 cm) in height, maintaining an erect position, and having a human form, thinly covered with short black hair, but I suspect that their height has been augmented by the fears of the Indians who greatly dread them."

EYEWITNESS ACCOUNT

A MELANCHOLY WHISTLE

In 1868, the explorer Charles Barrington Brown was on the Upper Mazaruni when he heard a most peculiar animal call. He described it as follows: "... a long, loud, and most melancholy whistle. Two or three times the whistle was repeated, sounding like that made by a human being, beginning in a high key and dying slowly and gradually away into a low one." Brown asked his local porters what had made the cry. They told him that it was the Didi, which they described as "a short, thickset, and powerful wild man whose body is covered with hair and who lives in the forest." Brown later met a man who had stumbled across a male and female Didi when out chopping timber one day. They had attacked him, scratching him badly, but he had defended himself with his axe and they had fled.

The de Loys Photograph

François de Loys was a Swiss geologist who, in 1917, was hired to explore the Sierra de Perijaa area along the Colombian–Venezuela border, partly to demarcate the border, but mostly to prospect for oil and gas. In 1920, while de Loys' team were camped near the Tarra River, southwest of Maracaibo, two large animals were seen approaching the camp through the undergrowth. De Loys at first thought they were bears, but then he saw that they were more like very large monkeys. What follows is de Loys' account of what happened.

The creatures were screaming, shouting, and thrashing at the bushes. They then tore branches off the undergrowth and started brandishing them overhead as if they were weapons. Working themselves up into a pitch of fury, the two creatures defecated into their hands and hurled the filth at the humans. Worried, de Loys and two other men picked up their rifles. One of the creatures dashed toward the humans. De Loys fired, dropping the animal dead in its tracks. The other creature vanished into the undergrowth.

De Loys and his team carried the dead animal back to camp, where they measured it and studied it thoroughly. The creature was 5 ft 2 in (157 cm) from its feet to the top of the head. It had no tail, and its limbs were stout and muscular compared to those of most monkeys, while its body was thinner from the front to the back than he had expected. De Loys sat the creature on a wooden storage crate, propped it upright with a stick, and took its photograph.

De Loys questioned his porters, who all came from the coastal regions. They said they had no idea what the creature was, but everyone agreed it was some sort of monkey. The beast was then skinned by the expedition cook, who was accustomed to dealing with all sorts of wild animals that had

This photograph, shot by François de Loys in 1920, continues to arouse controversy.

been shot for food. He cut off the head, boiled it to remove the flesh, and kept the skull. Unfortunately, the canoe carrying the skin and the skull overturned some weeks later and both items were lost to posterity.

In 1929, the anthropologist Georges Montandon visited de Loys at his Swiss home to research South American tribes. As he flicked through de Loys' notes, he spotted the photograph of the mystery monkey and asked what it was. De Loys retold the story of the encounter.

Montandon realized that the creature, as described by de Loys, was completely unknown to science. More strikingly, if the beast turned out to be an ape, it would be a landmark discovery because no apes were known to live in the Americas. Montandon published a description of the animal in the *Journal de la Société des Américanistes*. He gave the creature the scientific name of *Ameranthropoides loysi*, meaning Loys' American Ape.

But Montandan found himself alone. The idea of there being an ape in the Americas was opposed by nearly every zoologist of any repute. Several questioned the reality of the animal itself. Sir Arthur Keith, a prominent anthropologist, accused de Loys of fraud. He suggested that the photo was of a perfectly normal spider monkey with its tail hidden out of sight.

De Loys angrily denied the fraud. He repeatedly stated that, as a geologist, he had no idea that the presence of a large tailless primate was as remarkable as it turned out to be. He thought the beast was somewhat unusual, which is why he photographed it and measured it so carefully. If he had known how unusual the beast was, he would have taken more photographs and tried to preserve its skeleton. The zoological world remained unimpressed.

Reappraisal

In the intervening years, there has been a reappraisal of the photo and de Loys' claims. As Keith suggested, the animal in the photograph does indeed look like a spider monkey in terms of the shape of the nose and mouth, the proportions of the limbs, and the arrangement of the fingers and toes. However, there are differences. The face of the mystery animal is a rounded oval, not the roughly triangular shape more usual in spider monkeys.

TALE OF THE PARANORMAL

INOCENCIO'S STORY

In 1930, a hunter named Inocencio was spending the night in a tree near the headwaters of the Urubu River. About three hours after sunset, Inocencio heard a cry that sounded almost human. The cry came again, this time much closer. Peering into the undergrowth, Inocencio saw a creature moving beside a fallen tree. It then stepped out into the starlight. According to Inocencio, the thickset figure stood upright like a man, but was somehow different. It stared at Inocencio, then tipped its head back and roared. Inocencio fired, and the creature again roared loudly and started running forward as if to attack. Inocencio shot again, and this time he seemed to hit the creature, which sprang backward and then disappeared into the inky shadows. When dawn arrived, Inocencio clambered down. He found the clearing around the fallen tree spattered with blood, but there was no sign of the creature.

There is also the question of the creature's size. Researchers have worked out with reference to the height of the crate in the photo (which was of a standard size) that de Loys was correct in his measurement of the creature's height at 5 ft 2 in (157 cm). Spider monkeys, however, average 22 in (56 cm). It seems that de Loys and Montandon's claims are perhaps not as ridiculous as they appeared when Sir Arthur Keith wrote his damning critique.

The Millers' Expedition

In 1990, Marc Miller and his daughter Khryztian organized a five-person expedition up the Ventuari and Orinoco Rivers and their assorted tributaries in order to investigate reports of the Maricoxi. They took with them not only the de Loys photo, but also photographs of spider monkeys, chimpanzees, gorillas, and other primates. The plan was to find people who had seen the mystery giant monkey ape, collect detailed accounts, and then show them the photographs to see if they could identify what they had seen.

The expedition collected a number of eyewitness reports and managed to put together a picture of a giant monkey that tallied well with the de Loys photograph. According to the eyewitnesses, it stands about 5 feet (152 cm) tall, is covered in reddish-brown hair, and has arms that reach down to its knees. It eats fruits, particularly the fruits of the chonta palm, and is found most often in the hills at altitudes of over 2,000 ft (610 m). The creature is apparently not common, but neither is it particularly rare. It is supposedly wary of humans, and, while it will usually flee, it might become aggressive if cornered. The Millers returned from the dense forests certain of the reality of the giant monkey or ape, but the scientific establishment remains unconvinced.

This depiction of a South American man-ape is based on eyewitness reports.

ASIAN WILD MEN

There have been hundreds of reports coming out of Central Asia about a creature that is neither fully human nor entirely animal. It goes by many names, depending on the language of the people who encounter it. Among the terms for this wild man are Abnuaaya, Barmanu, Bekk-Bok, Biabin-Guli, Gul-Biavan, Guli-Avan, Golub-Yavan, Kaptar, Kra-Dhan, Ksy Gyik, Mirygdy, Mulen, and Voita. However, researchers have needed a general term when referring to these creatures. Those studying reports from China tend to call the beast the Yeren, while those looking at reports from Mongolia and the former Soviet Union call it Almas, or sometimes Almasti.

What Is It and Where Does It Live?

Theories abound about what the legendary creature might be. Some researchers speculate that, if it exists, it may be an unknown primate. Others argue that it may be a bear or a monkey, and still others suggest it could be a creature halfway between ape and human.

Studying the Almas or Yeren has been made more difficult by the inaccessibility of the places in which it is said to live. The largest of these are the forested mountains and uplands around the Tien Shan mountain range that straddles the borders of Russia, Mongolia, and China. Reports also come from the mountains of China's Hubei province as well as the more remote regions of the Caucasus Mountains. All of these areas are difficult to reach and lacking in good roads.

Ivlov's Encounter

One of the first outsiders to take an interest in the Almas-Yeren was a Russian doctor by the name of Ivan Ivlov. In the autumn of 1963, he was travelling through the Altai Mountains, a northern spur of the Tien Shan, when he spotted three figures some distance away on a mountain slope. Ivlov took out his binoculars to get a better view. He later reported that the shape of the figures, and the way they moved, was human but that they were covered in hair. There was a male, a slightly smaller female, and a child. The creatures seemed to be digging, perhaps for roots to eat. When they saw Ivlov and his caravan, they moved off. They rounded a rock crag and disappeared from sight. Ivlov was puzzled and turned

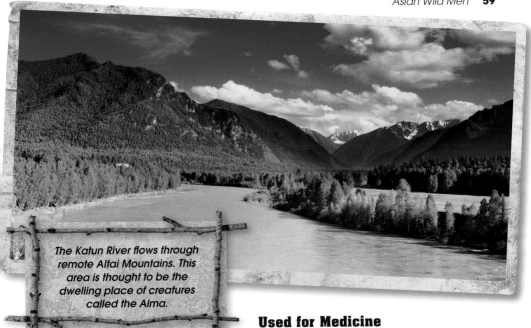

The Katun River flows through remote Altai Mountains. This area is thought to be the dwelling place of creatures called the Alma.

to his Mongolian companions. They told him that the figures were wild men. They explained that the wild men were not really humans, but were more like animals.

Ivlov was intrigued, and, throughout the rest of his journey, he quizzed his companions about these mysterious wild men. He learned that the local herdsmen did not think that the humanlike creatures were at all mysterious or unusual: they were just another part of the local wildlife. One local told Ivlov of the time an Almas male had scooped up a juvenile when it spotted the Mongolian approaching. As the adult Almas strode off, the youngster peered over its shoulder at the human, then stuck its tongue out and made faces – a remarkably human response.

Used for Medicine

Published in the Qing Dynasty in around the year 1664 was a book entitled *The Mirror of Medicine*. It was a compendium of wild animals to be found in northern China and Mongolia and suggested ways their parts could be used for treating illnesses.

EYEWITNESS ACCOUNT

WILD PEOPLE OF THE MOUNTAINS

The earliest known written reference to an Asian wild man comes from the book written in the 1430s by a Bavarian nobleman called Hans Schiltberger.
"In the mountains live wild people, who have nothing in common with normal human beings. A pelt of fur covers the entire body of these creatures. Only the hands and face are free of hair. They run around the hills like animals and eat foliage and grass and whatever else they can find."

Among the assorted wildlife, it included an entry for the "wild man": "The wild man lives in the northern mountains, and his origins are like that of the bear. His body resembles that of a man, and he has enormous strength. His meat may be eaten to treat mental disease. His gall cures jaundice."

Alongside the text was a small illustration. It showed a basically human figure standing on a rock with its left arm upraised. The entire body of the creature, except for its feet and hands, was covered in dense fur. Even the eyes and the mouth were surrounded by hair.

Wild Captive

In 1910, a Kazakh herdsman told Russian zoologist V.A. Khaklov that he recalled having seen a wild woman in his youth. He said that she had been captured by some farmers and was being kept chained up when he saw her. The herdsman said that the woman was usually quiet, but would screech and bare her teeth if approached. He said that she had a most peculiar way of lying down to sleep. She rested on her knees and elbows with her forehead on the ground and with her hands folded over the back of her head. The herdsman recalled that the wild woman ate raw meat and vegetables and that, when drinking, she would lap like a dog. She was apparently released after a few days and fled back to the forests.

Zhamtsarano's Research

Professor Tsyben Zhamtsarano was a Russian-educated Mongolian researcher of the Alamas. In 1907, Zhamtsarano interviewed dozens of Mongolian nomads who claimed to have encountered the wild men. He made detailed notes of their reports and employed a local artist to work with the nomads to produce a series of pictures of the creatures. He also created a map of the Tien Shan region and marked on it each sighting, together with the date it was

EYEWITNESS ACCOUNT

HAIRY CORPSE

In 1980, a man working for the Mongolian government was travelling through Bulgan when he came across a dead body. At first, he took it to be that of a human. Then he looked more closely:

"I approached and saw a hairy corpse of a robust humanlike creature dried and half buried by sand. I had never seen such a humanlike being before, covered by camel-color brownish-yellow short hairs, and I recoiled, although in my native land in Sinkiang I had seen many dead men killed in battle. The dead thing was not a bear or ape, and, at the same time, it was not a man like Mongol or Kazakh or Chinese and Russian. The hairs of its head were longer than on its body. The skin was darkened and shrivelled like a hide of a dead camel."

made. Unfortunately, his archives are believed to have been destroyed during the German siege of Leningrad in 1941–2.

In the 1960s, one of Zhamtsarano's research assistants, Dordji Meiren, recalled some details of the research. He said that Zhamtsarano believed that the numbers of reports had declined drastically after about 1890, and that by 1925 the Almas appeared to have become extinct across as much as half of its range. He also remembered being shown a skin of an Almas male. He said it seemed to be that of a human a little over 5 ft (152 cm) tall, except that it was covered in dense reddish-brown curly hair. The hair on the scalp was much longer and densely matted, but the face was hairless around the eyes and the mouth. Short, curly hair grew on the cheeks and the forehead. The fingers and toes, Meiren said, carried nails that looked identical to those of a human. He did not know what had become of the hide.

Koffman Expedition

In 1992, the first serious expedition to investigate the Almas was led into the Tien Shan area by Dr. Marie-Jeanne Koffman, a Russian anatomist and mountain climber. The expedition collected more than 500 eyewitness accounts, including descriptions of Almas families. Although no Almas was captured, nor even seen by expedition members, they did come back with some droppings and hairs that the locals said had come from the Almas.

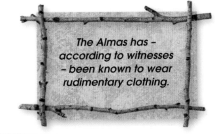

The Almas has – according to witnesses – been known to wear rudimentary clothing.

The hairs could not be matched to any known animal, but they might have come from a primate. The droppings contained food remains that showed that the animal that had made them was omnivorous, but in shape and texture they were unlike those of a bear – the only large omnivore known to live in the area.

Hairy Giants

In 1925, Major General Mikhail Topilski was commanding a regiment of the Red Army against anti-Communist forces in the Pamir Mountains, southwest of the Tien Shan. A captured enemy soldier told him that he and his companions had been attacked by a band of gigantic hairy men armed with clubs, and he was the only survivor. The wounded man showed Topilski the site of the battle, a cave beside a glacier. The bodies of the man's five comrades were found, and so was the body of one of the "hairy giants." Topilski's report continued: "At first glance, I thought the body was that of an ape. It was covered with hair all over. But I knew there were no apes in the Pamirs. Also, the body itself looked very much like that of a man. We tried pulling the hair, to see if it was just a hide used for disguise, but found that it was the creature's own natural hair.... Our doctor ... made a long and thorough inspection of the body, and it was clear that it was not a human."

Too Human to Kill

In 1948, M.A. Stonin, a geologist, was prospecting near Tien Shan. One morning. he awoke to cries by his guides that the horses were being stolen. Stonin grabbed his rifle and headed outside to find a figure standing by the horses. According to Stonin, it had long red hair all over its body. The creature moved off at Stonin's shouts, and he chased after it. It was so humanlike, though, that Stonin couldn't bring himself to shoot it, and the thing escaped.

Reports from China

Chinese tales of the wild men, or Yeren, go back to the 9th century CE, when the historian Li Yanshow stated that

EYEWITNESS ACCOUNT

BIG FOOTPRINTS

In June 1997, Wang Fangchen, head of China's Committee for Research on Strange and Rare Creatures, announced: "Hundreds of very large footprints resembling those of a man – but much larger – have been seen in the forests of the mountainous Shennongjia National Park in central Hubei province. We have made preliminary conclusions that they were left by two animals walking on two legs. The biggest footprint is 15 in (37 centimetres) long, very similar to that of a man but is quite (a bit) larger than a man's, and is different from the footprints of a bear or any other identified animals." He added that the creature that made the footprints weighed an estimated 440 lb (200 kg).

The Yeren appears to be significantly more ape-like than the Almas.

Illinois, claimed to have seen the corpse of one of these creatures in 1940. He was driving to Tianshui in Gansu province when he heard gunfire and then came across a group of soldiers standing around a strange body. It was a female, humanlike creature, about 6 ft 6 in (197 cm) tall and covered with a coat of thick, grayish-red hair about 1.25 in (3 cm) long. The hair on its head was about

the forests of Hubei province sheltered a band of such creatures. In the 18th century, the Chinese poet Yuan Mei wrote about creatures in the wild regions of Shanxi province, calling them "monkeylike, yet not monkeylike."

The stories have continued into modern times. Wang Zelin, a graduate of the biology department of Northwestern University in Chicago,

12 in (30 cm) long, but the hair on its face was shorter. Its cheek bones were prominent and its lips jutted out.

In 1957, a middle-school teacher of biology in Zhejiang province claimed to have obtained the hands and feet of a "man-bear" killed by local peasants. He believed that they might possibly belong to an enormous monkey of some unknown kind.

The Caucasus Mountains are another area associated with sightings of ape-men.

The Kaptar

Although the majority of Almas reports come from the Tien Shan and nearby regions, others have emerged from the Caucasus. Here the creatures are known as the Kaptar. One of the first reports of a Kaptar to be made by an outsider came from Russian zoologist K.A. Satunin in 1899. One evening, while Satunin was travelling through the Talysh hills of Georgia, he allegedly saw a humanlike figure that seemed to be covered in hair. The sighting lasted only a few seconds before the creature dashed off into dense undergrowth. Satunin's guides told him that the creature had been a forest woman – a Biaban Guli or Kaptar.

Zana

According to another account, a Kaptar woman was captured alive in the Caucasus Mountains some time around 1840. She was described as being covered all over in dark, red-brown hair, beneath which she had an equally dark skin. Her body was broad and muscular, as were her limbs, and she had particularly big hands. The Kaptar woman could not talk and never learned to speak the local language, though she could make herself understood at a fairly basic level with hand gestures. She called herself something that sounded like "Zana," so that was the name that she was given. Over the years that followed, Zana was sold or given to various owners. She apparently died in the 1880s.

Forest People

Another researcher active in the 1960s was John Colarusso. After speaking at great length to Caucasian hill men, he became convinced of the reality of the Kaptar. He spoke to several men who claimed to have traded with the creatures they called "forest people." One hunter said that he would frequently take beads and shiny bangles or sequins with him when visiting the high valleys. These he would spread out on the ground by his camp to attract the forest people.

He said that the first sign of the creatures would be when a large male was seen hovering about near the forest edge. Then the male would come forward, while females and children could be glimpsed hiding in the undergrowth. The male would bring fruits or roots from the forest to exchange for the trinkets. Occasionally, the females or young males might also approach. None made any effort to talk to him, though they would often jabber to each other in some strange way, using hand signs and facial expressions. He reported that they could be sly and cunning. If he did not keep his eyes open, the forest people would try to steal his trinkets.

EYEWITNESS ACCOUNT

"EYES OF AN ANIMAL"

In 1941, a Russian officer named Vargen Karapetyan was fighting the German invaders near Buinakst when some partisans asked him what they should do with a rather unusual prisoner. Karapetyan later wrote:

"I entered a shed with two members of the local authorities.... I can still see the creature as it stood before me, a male, naked and barefooted. And it was doubtlessly a man, because its entire shape was human. The chest, back, and shoulders, however, were covered with shaggy hair of a dark brown color.... His eyes told me nothing. They were dull and empty – the eyes of an animal. And he seemed to me like an animal and nothing more."

From the accounts given by Colarusso, it seemed that these forest people stood a bit over 5 ft (152 cm) in height and were covered in slightly curly brown or reddish hair, which was much longer on the top of the head. Their faces were described as being pushed forward, indicating that the chin and forehead both sloped backward. They walked upright like humans and were agile and immensely strong. The Kaptar were not aggressive, but would fight ferociously if they felt threatened or if a human got too close to their young.

ORANG PENDEK

Somewhere in the mountainous forests of southern Sumatra is said to live the Orang Pendek – the "short man." The local villagers of the more densely forested regions appear to take the creature for granted, much as they do the tiger and the rhinoceros.

Reports from Europeans

The first reference to this creature to be written by an outsider was made in 1917 by a Dr. Edward Jacobson. He said that he had been camped near Boekit Kaba when the local men he had hired to hunt meat for him came strolling in to announce that they had just passed an Orang Pendek. It had been looking for insect larvae in a fallen log. They

EYEWITNESS ACCOUNT

NERVOUS ENCOUNTER

In 1923, a Dutch explorer named Van Herwaarden was out hunting wild pigs on the island of Poleloe Rimau, off Sumatra, when he saw something unusual sitting in a tree:

"I discovered a dark and hairy creature on a branch. The front of its body was pressed tightly against the tree. It looked as if it were trying to make itself inconspicuous and felt that it was about to be discovered. I laid my gun on the ground and tried to get nearer the animal.... The creature lifted itself a little from the branch and leaned over the side so that I could then see its hair, its forehead, and a pair of eyes which stared at me. Its movements had at first been slow and cautious, but, as soon as the thing saw me, the whole situation changed. It became nervous and trembled all over.... There was nothing repulsive or ugly about the face, nor was it at all ape-like, although the quick nervous movements of its eyes and mouth were very like those of a monkey in distress. I began to talk in a calm and friendly way to the beast as if I were soothing a frightened dog or horse, but it did not make much difference. When I raised my gun, I heard a plaintive 'hu-hu,' which was at once answered by similar calls from the forest nearby. I laid my gun on the ground and climbed into the tree again. The beast ran very fast along a branch, then dropped 10 feet (3 m) to the ground. By the time I reached my gun, it was 30 yards (27 m) away and running fast, giving a sort of whistle. Many people may think me childish if I say that, when I saw its flying hair in the sights, I did not pull the trigger. I suddenly felt that I was going to commit murder."

This CGI reconstruction shows the sighting by Van Herwaarden of an Orang Pendek sitting eating in a tree.

said that the creature had run off when it had seen them. After further questioning, Jacobson learned that the creature had run off on its hind legs. Jacobson thought this odd because the only apes he knew of, gibbons and orangutans, would have swung off through the trees. He went to investigate and allegedly found a footprint that looked exactly like that of a human, except that it was very small.

Jacobson's report prompted a separate account from another European living in Sumatra, L.C. Westenenk. He stated that a friend of his had been leading a gang of workmen into the forest near Loeboek Salasik to cut timber when they came across what he described as: "... a large creature, low on its feet, which ran like a man and was about to cross the path. It was very hairy and was not an orangutan. Its face was not like an ordinary man's. It silently and gravely gave the men a disagreeable stare and ran calmly away. The workmen ran faster in the opposite direction."

WHAT DOES THE ORANG PENDEK LOOK LIKE?

Those who claim to have seen the Orang Pendek say it looks like a short human, though with some clear differences. It has a light covering of dark fur that is thicker on the limbs than on the body. The top of the head carries a mane of much longer hair that grows down the back, at least as far as the shoulder blades and perhaps to the waist. Its forehead is high, and its ears are like those of a human, while the body is stocky and muscular, with a prominent pot-belly.

Its arms are a bit longer than those of a human, but not as elongated as are those of a gibbon. The creature walks on its hind legs alone, and the few footprints that have been found and cast in plaster show that its foot is very like that of a human, with an arch and five toes arranged along the front edge. In size, the footprints are about the same as those made by a 7- or 8-year-old human child, but rather wider at the front and with a robust ball joint behind the big toe.

Debbie Martyr's Search

In July 1989, a British reporter named Deborah Martyr travelled to Sumatra's Mount Kerinici area of dense, largely unexplored rainforest to seek out animals to photograph. Her guide explained where to find tigers, rhinoceros, and other creatures. Then, quite casually, he pointed to the area of land east of Mount Tujuh and remarked that if they had more time they could go there to see Orang Pendek, but that there was not really time, and, in any case the creatures were rare and very shy.

At the time, Martyr thought the guide was using a local name for a type of gibbon. Gradually, she realized that he and others who said that they had met the Orang Pendek were referring to something altogether different. Back in London, Martyr researched the term and discovered the Orang Pendek was a cryptid ape supposed to be rather humanlike, but that there was no hard evidence to support its existence. Realizing that the local villagers she had spoken to considered the creature to be very real indeed, Martyr went straight back to search for the Orang Pendek.

She has been on the trail of the legendary animal ever since, and what is known — or at least claimed — of this cryptid is largely due to her work. In 1999, Debbie Martyr claims she was rewarded for her persistence by a sighting of what she described as a "bipedal half-ape, half-gibbon looking orang pendek."

Recent Research

In 2003, researchers Adam Davies and Andrew Sanderson found hairs and made a cast of a footprint, seemingly belonging to an unknown primate. Examination of the footprint cast

that are operated when something moves within their field of vision. To date, however, nothing definitive has been photographed.

A Threatened Species?

If the Orang Pendek exists, the evidence suggests it was formerly widely distributed over the rainforest-covered hills of southern Sumatra. The island covers almost 200,000 sq miles (518,000 sq km), and even today there are large stretches of virgin forest. However, the growth of the oil and timber industries has led to the construction of a growing network of roads through the interior. As well as loggers and oil companies, ordinary people are using these access routes for hunting, pushing into many areas that were previously remote. Perhaps because of this, encounters with the Orang Pendek are now reported from an increasingly small area. By the 1990s, reported encounters were coming only from an area between Bangko and Mount Kerinici.

revealed that it came from an ape that had features of both the human and chimpanzee foot, but that the cast matched no known primate. The hairs were studied by the Austrian specialist Dr. Hans Brunner. He concluded that they were from a primate, but he could not assign them to any known species.

In 2005, the National Geographic Society set up a project in the Mount Tenici region based on the use of camera traps. These are cameras

THE AUSTRALIAN YOWIE

For many decades, the wooded hills of eastern Australia have yielded reports of a creature that is sometimes called the Hairy Fellah but is more commonly termed the Yowie. The latter name grew out of one of the many Aboriginal terms for this creature in New South Wales (NSW). Other terms for the creature, from the various Aboriginal languages, include gulaga, thoolalgarl, doolagarl, myngawin, and joogabinna.

Aboriginal Stories

Traditional Aboriginal stories about this creature often feature elements of the supernatural. For instance, the Dulugars of the Suggan Buggan can allegedly fly through the air, and the Quinkin of the Yalanji people is apparently a demon taller than a tree. The Yaroma, meanwhile, are said to have mouths so large that they can swallow men whole.

As European settlers began overrunning Aboriginal lands, they began to hear reports of Yowies. Black Harry, a leader of the Ngunnawal people, reported that in about 1847 he had seen a group of warriors attack and kill one of these creatures on the banks of the Murrumbidgee River. He said that the mystery creature was "like a black man, but covered all over with gray hair."

EYEWITNESS ACCOUNT

UNEARTHLY LOOKING BEING

In 1876, no fewer than nine Europeans were on the Laachlan River when they saw, according to one of them: "... an inhuman, unearthly looking being, bearing in every way the shape of a man, with a big red face, hands, and legs covered with long shaggy hair. The head was covered with dark, grissly hair, the face with shaggy, dark hair, the back and belly with hair of a lighter color. This devil-devil, or whatever it may be called, doubled round and fled."

European Reports

A number of Europeans began to claim sightings of the hairy creatures, too. In 1882, H.J. McCooey came across a creature near Batemans Bay, NSW. "My attention was attracted by the cries of a number of birds, which were pursuing and darting at it. It was partly upright, looking up at the birds, blinking its eyes, and making a chattering sound. The creature was nearly 5 feet (152 cm) tall and covered with very long black hair which was dirty red ... color about the throat and breast. Its eyes, which were small and restless, were partly hidden by matted hair. The length of the arms seemed out of proportion. It would probably have weighed about 8 stone (112 lbs; 51 kg)." McCooey threw a stone at it, and the creature ran off.

In 1912, Charles Harper was camping out on Currickbilly Ridge, NSW, with two companions when they heard a "low rumbling growl" coming from the darkness. One of the men threw a handful of twigs onto the embers of the camp fire, causing flames to spring up and illuminate the creature that had been making the noise. Harper later recorded it as being "a huge man-like animal growling, grimacing, and thumping his breast with his huge, hand-like paws. I should say its height would be 5ft 8in to 5ft 10in (173–179 cm). Its body, legs, and arms were covered with long brownish-red hair, which shook with every quivering movement of its body.

"The hair on its shoulders and back parts appeared in the light of the fire to be jet black and long; but what struck me as most extraordinary was the apparently human shape, but still so very different. The body frame was enormous, indicating immense strength and power of endurance. The arms and forepaws were long and large, and very muscular, being covered with shorter hair. The head and face were small but very human. The eyes were large, dark, and piercing, deeply set. A most horrible mouth was ornamented with two large and long canine teeth. When the jaws were closed, they protruded over the lower lip." Harper added that the creature stood watching the men for a few seconds, then dropped onto all fours and raced off into the bush.

Reports indicate that the Yowie is rather more human than some of its fellow cryptid humanoids.

The Harper sighting of 1912 produced some of the most detailed early descriptions of the Yowie.

Is the Yowie a Giant Wombat?

In 1987, Stan Pappin was felling trees near Goothie, Queensland, when he heard a large animal approaching. The creature emerged from the undergrowth about 18 ft (5.5 m) away. Pappin thought the beast looked very much like a big bear, but with a humanlike head. He said its muzzle was very short and the ears were humanlike. It had a rather snub nose, which he described as clearly defined and free of hair, while its chin was receding. A very stocky and muscular neck joined its head to its body. The creature had approached on all fours, but it now stood up on its hind legs. Pappin reported that its front legs hung down in front, like those of a bear, but its feet were more like hands than paws. After regarding Pappin for a few seconds, the creature turned, took a few steps, then dropped down on all fours and ran off at speed.

Pappin's account was strangely reminiscent of a reported encounter from 1893. This concerned a "giant wombat" that had been killed by a Mr. Arthur Martin on October 28, and carried into Braidwood, NSW. The animal had weighed 98 lb (44 kg) and its tailless body had measured 4 ft

On August 7, 1970, Rex Gilroy was resting in a bush area near Katoomba when he allegedly saw a hairy, humanlike creature walk across a clearing only a few yards away from where he was seated. This experience prompted Gilroy to look into Yowie reports, and he soon became convinced that a species of giant ape-men lived in the Blue Mountains. He established a natural history museum and spent his time trying to prove his ideas. He sometimes made claims that were later disproved, but he did succeed in establishing the Yowie as a subject for research by others interested in cryptozoology. That, in turn, made people more willing to report encounters with the Yowie.

Apart from their size, the creatures killed by Martin and allegedly seen by Pappin are not too dissimilar to the commonly seen 3-ft (91-cm) long wombats. Furthermore, fossils of enormous wombat-like creatures have been found in southeastern Australia. The Diprotodon was about 10 ft (304 cm) long, and it died out only about 15,000 years ago. Some researchers believe it is possible that a large type of wombat might have survived in remote areas.

What Is the Yowie?

This raises the question of what exactly the Yowie is. Perhaps influenced by reports of the Sasquatch, modern researchers and witnesses have tended to emphasize the animal's supposedly apelike characteristics. However, not all witnesses actually describe an apelike creature. Something more like a giant wombat would fit the descriptions just as well in some cases.

For instance, in 2004, Margo Braithwaite said she saw a very tall, dark figure standing motionless in scrub near her home. She could see only the silhouette because it was a dark, rainy day, and the figure disappeared when she went to get her shoes on to investigate. However, by measuring a tree beside which the creature had been standing, she estimated it to be about 7 ft (213 cm) tall.

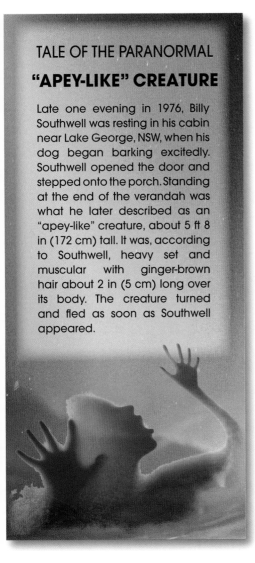

TALE OF THE PARANORMAL

"APEY-LIKE" CREATURE

Late one evening in 1976, Billy Southwell was resting in his cabin near Lake George, NSW, when his dog began barking excitedly. Southwell opened the door and stepped onto the porch. Standing at the end of the verandah was what he later described as an "apey-like" creature, about 5 ft 8 in (172 cm) tall. It was, according to Southwell, heavy set and muscular with ginger-brown hair about 2 in (5 cm) long over its body. The creature turned and fled as soon as Southwell appeared.

(122 cm) from head to rump. Its head was like that of a bear, but shorter, and it was covered with stout hair of a pale brown color. The four legs were slender and ended in feet that looked like the hands of a man with overgrown fingernails. This creature had also approached on all fours, then stood up on its hind legs when it got close to Martin.

Other reports suggest a creature that is definitely more apelike or human in appearance. In August 2001, a Mrs. Laidley was driving near Mulgowies, Queensland, when she allegedly saw an "orangutan-like animal with a bare bottom" cross the road. It was, she said, about as big as an Alsatian dog. Not too long afterward, in April 2003, Jason Cole reported seeing a gorillalike creature staring at him from nearby undergrowth while he was felling trees near Ormeau, Queensland. Cole said that when he looked at it, the creature slipped out of sight, but he could hear it moving about for some time.

Unreliable Witnesses

What is striking about many Yowie reports is that the sightings are generally in poor light or last for only a few seconds. Under such circumstances, it is remarkably easy for a person to be mistaken, especially if they have already heard about the possible existence of a cryptid such as the Yowie.

A 1987 Yowie case makes the point that eyewitnesses are not always reliable. On February 22, the *Brisbane Mail* carried a report of a Yowie sighting. Frank Burns, Phyllis Kenny, and Mrs. Kenny's four grandchildren were driving across the outback near Alice Springs when they stopped at a waterhole for a rest. Mr. Burns lit a fire and began brewing up a cup of tea,

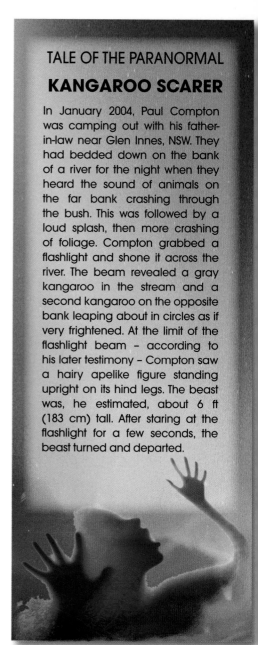

TALE OF THE PARANORMAL
KANGAROO SCARER

In January 2004, Paul Compton was camping out with his father-in-law near Glen Innes, NSW. They had bedded down on the bank of a river for the night when they heard the sound of animals on the far bank crashing through the bush. This was followed by a loud splash, then more crashing of foliage. Compton grabbed a flashlight and shone it across the river. The beam revealed a gray kangaroo in the stream and a second kangaroo on the opposite bank leaping about in circles as if very frightened. At the limit of the flashlight beam – according to his later testimony – Compton saw a hairy apelike figure standing upright on its hind legs. The beast was, he estimated, about 6 ft (183 cm) tall. After staring at the flashlight for a few seconds, the beast turned and departed.

while Mrs. Kenny got out a picnic lunch and the children ran about playing games. Suddenly a terrifying figure leapt out of a large, open-topped water storage tank. Mrs. Kenny later described

sort of loped along. It had big eyes, a large forehead, and it was all red around the mouth." The family fled to their vehicle and drove off at high speed. The last they saw was the "Yowie" trying to grab the back of their vehicle. They reported the matter to the police, then to the press.

A few weeks later the newspapers published a follow-up report from the police. Two patrolmen were sent out to investigate and found the "Yowie" sitting by the side of the road. He turned out to be completely human and well known to locals. Franjo Jurcevic was a large, heavily bearded Yugoslav immigrant who had taken to living wild in the area some years earlier. He survived by eating wild foods, supplemented by groceries bought at a local store with his welfare money.

the figure as "... a man-like animal covered with hair and standing at least 6 ft 6 in (2 meters) tall.

"You can tell the difference between a man and a beast," she continued, "and that was no man. There are some things that you just can't explain, that are just scary, and that was one of them. I nearly died." One of the older children said: "It ran like a gorilla. Its arms hung down at its sides, and it just

GLOSSARY

anatomist An expert in anatomy, the science concerned with the bodily structure of humans, animals, and other living organisms.

anthropologist An expert in anthropology, the study of humankind.

artifact An object made by a human being, typically an item of cultural or historical interest.

biomechanics The study of the mechanical laws relating to the movement or structure of living organisms.

biotechnologists Scientists who study the natural world and apply its lessons in the development of technology.

captor One who has captured a person, animal, or thing.

carcass The dead body of an animal.

carnivore An animal that feeds on flesh.

carrion The decaying flesh of dead animals.

cast A three-dimensional shape, such as a footprint, made by shaping a material (such as plaster of Paris) in a mold of that shape.

col The lowest point of a ridge or saddle between two mountain peaks, typically affording a pass from one side of a mountain range to another.

coniferous Relating to a tree that bears cones and evergreen needlelike or scalelike leaves.

credible Offering reasonable grounds for being believed; believable.

cryptid A creature that appears in stories, rumors, and legends, but whose existence is not recognized by science.

cryptozoologist A person who studies cryptids.

deduce To infer from a general purpose; to determine by reasoning and logic.

fur trapper A person who traps wild animals for their fur.

generic Relating to a class or group of things; not specific.

geologist An expert in geology, the science that deals with the earth's physical structure and substance, its history, and the processes that act on it.

gibbon A small, slender tree-dwelling ape with long powerful arms and loud hooting calls, native to the forests of Southeast Asia.

glacier A slowly moving mass or river of ice formed by the accumulation and compacting of snow on mountains or near the poles.

grizzly bear A large species of brown bear native to North America.

hominid A primate of the family *Hominidae* that includes humans and their extinct ancestors.

Homo erectus An extinct species of hominid.

lumberjack A person who fells trees, cuts them into logs, or transports them to a sawmill.

mammary glands The milk-producing glands of female mammals.

naturalist An expert in natural history, the scientific study of animals or plants.

Neanderthal An extinct species of hominid that was widely distributed in ice-age Europe between c. 120,000–35,000 years ago.

nomad A member of a people having no permanent home, who travel from place to place to find fresh pasture for their livestock.

ominous Foreboding or foreshadowing evil; being or exhibiting an omen.

omnivore An animal or person that eats food of both plant and animal origin.

orangutan A large, mainly solitary tree-dwelling ape with long reddish hair, long arms, and hooked hands and feet, native to Borneo and Sumatra.

outhouse A small building, often used for storage, built close to but separate from a house.

palaeontologist An expert in palaeontology, the branch of science concerned with fossil animals and plants.

phenomenon A fact or situation that is observed to exist or happen.

plaster of Paris A soft white substance made by the addition of water to powdered gypsum, which hardens when dried. It is used for making sculptures and casts.

primate A mammal of an order that includes monkeys, apes, and humans. They are distinguished by having hands, handlike feet, and forward-facing eyes.

prospector Someone who searches for mineral deposits, such as gold, by means of experimental drilling and excavation.

remote Far removed in space, time, or relation; out-of-the-way; secluded.

Sherpa A member of a Himalayan people living on the borders of Nepal and Tibet, renowned for their skill in mountaineering.

skunk A cat-sized American mammal of the weasel family, with distinctive black-and-white-striped fur. When threatened, it squirts a spray of foul-smelling liquid from its anal glands toward its attacker.

snuff box A small ornamental box for holding snuff. Snuff is a powdered form of tobacco that is sniffed up the nostril rather than smoked.

striation Linear marks, ridges, or grooves on a surface, often one of a number of similar, parallel features.

zoologist An expert in zoology, the scientific study of the behavior, structure, classification, and distribution of animals.

FURTHER INFORMATION

Anatomy of a Beast: Obsession and Myth on the Trail of Bigfoot, by Michael McLeod (Berkeley, CA: University of California Press, 2009).

Bigfoot and Other Mysterious Creatures, by John Townsend (New York, NY: Crabtree Publishing Co., 2008).

Bigfoot Caught on Film: And Other Monster Sightings (24/7: Science Behind the Scenes: Mystery Files), by Michael Teitelbaum (New York, NY: Childrens Press, 2008).

Bigfoot Observer's Field Manual: A Practical and Easy-to-Follow Step-by-Step Guide to Your Very Own Face-to-Face Encounter with a Legend, by Robert W. Morgan (Ravensdale, WA: Pine Woods Press, 2008).

Bigfoot: The Life and Times of a Legend, by Joshua Blu Buhs (Chicago, IL: University of Chicago Press, 2010).

Sasquatch: True-Life Encounters with Legendary Ape-Men, by Rupert Matthews (Edison, NJ: Chartwell Books, 2008).

Searching for Bigfoot (Mystery Explorers), by Stewart Cowley and Greg Cox (New York, NY: Rosen Publishing, 2012).

Supposedly True Stories of Bigfoot Sightings, by Lance A. Hobday (Charleston, SC: CreateSpace, 2010).

The Weiser Guide to Cryptozoology: Werewolves, Dragons, Skyfish, Lizard Men, and Other Fascinating Creatures Real and Mysterios, by Deena West Budd (San Francisco, CA: Weiser Books, 2010).

Yetis, Sasquatch, and Hairy Giants, by David Hatcher Childress (Kempton, IL: Adventures Unlimited Press, 2010).

WEB SITES

Due to the changing nature of Internet links, Rosen Publishing has developed an online list of Web sites related to the subject of this book. This site is updated regularly. Please use this link to access the list:

http://www.rosenlinks.com/pfiles/big

INDEX

Numbers in **bold** *refer to illustrations.*

Abominable Snowman *see* Yeti
Allen, Betty 12, 13
Almas 58-59, 60, 61, **61**, 64
Ameranthropoides loysi 55
Anseering 49, **49**
ape-men 4-11, 6, 12, 15, 17, 52, 53, **57**, 72
Asian wild men 58-65
  footprints 62

Baird, Donald 31
Bancroft, Edward 53
Battle of Ape Canyon 4-6
Beck, Fred 4-6
Bigfoot 4-11, **10**, 12-13, 14, 15, 16, **16**, 17, 18-19, **18**, 20-24, **21**, 30-35, 43
  fakes and hoaxes 15, 20-21, **21**, 25, 29, 30-31, **30**
  film about (*also see* specific named footage) 20-23, **21**, 24, 25, 26, 27, 28-29
  footprints 6, 9, 12, 13, **13**, 14, **14**, 15, 16, 20, 22, 23-24, **23**, 26, 29, **29**, 30-33, **30**, **32**, "nests" 34-35
  newspaper reports about 12, 13, 14
  scientific analysis of evidence 25, 26, 27
  snow mounds 35
Bigfoot Field Researchers Organization (BFRO) 33
Black Harry 70
Bluff Creek 12-15, **14**, 20
Bourtsev, Igor 26
Braithwaite, Margo 73

Brown, Charles Barrington 54
Brunner, Hans 69
Burns, Frank 74
Byrne, Peter 47

Chambers, John 27
Chapman, George and Jennie 9, **9**
Colarusso, John 65
Cole, Jason 74
Coleman, Loren 41
Compton, Paul 74
Crew, Jerry 12, 13, 15, 31
cryptids 5, 32, 52, 53, 68, 74, 76
cryptozoologists 28, 43, 76

Dahinden, René 14, 20, 22, 25
Dakhu 48
Davies, Adam 68
Didi 53, 54

Eastern Bigfoot 43

Fangchen, Wang 62
Fawcett, Percy 52
Florida Ape *see* Skunk Ape
Ford case 42-43
Freeman footage 21
Freeman, Paul **29**

Gensheng, Pang 50
Gigantopithecus 51
Gilroy, Rex 72
Gimlin, Bob 20-23, **23**, 24, 27
gold prospectors 4-5, 76
Green, John 14, 20, 22, 24, 25

Grieve, Don 25, 26, 27

Harper, Charles 71
Hatfield, Robert 18
Herwaarden, Van 66, **67**
Hillary, Edmund 46-47
Hodgson, B.H. 45
Howard-Bury, Colonel 46
Humboldt, Alexander von 53

Inocencio 56
Ivlov, Ivan 58-59

Jacobson, Edward 66-67
Jenkins, Bud 18-19
Jurcevic, Franjo 75

Kaptar 64-65
Karapetyan, Vargen 65
Keith, Arthur 56, 57
Kenny, Phyllis 74-75
Khaklov, V. A. 60
Koffman, Marie-Jeanne 61
Krantz, Grover 29, 33

León, Pedro de Cieza de 53
Loys, François de 54, 55, **55**, 56, 57

MacDonald, Mary 45
Manitoba footage 21
Maricoxi 6, 52-57
Martin, Arthur 72-73
Martyr, Deborah 68
McCooey, H.J. 70-71
Mei, Yuan 63
Meiren, Dordji 61
Meldrum, Jeff 33

Miller, Marc 57

Mills, Joan 43

Mono Grande 53

Montandon, Georges 55, 56, 57

Moskowitz, Kathy 34-35

Muchalat Harry 7

native peoples 4

Newman, Henry 46

Nima, Pasang 48-49

Orang Pendek 6, 66-69, **67**, **69**

  footprints 68-69

Osbun, H.C. 41

Ostman, Albert 7-8, 10-11, 34

Pappin, Stan 72, 73

Patterson, Roger 20-23, **21**, **23**, 24, 25, 26, 27

Planet of the Apes 27, **27**

Redwoods Footage 21

Roe, William 11

Ruby Creek Incident 9

Ryan, Mary 43

Sanderson, Andrew 68

Sasquatch *see* Bigfoot

Satunin, K.A. 64

Schiltberger, Hans 59

Sheppard, David 48

Shipton, Eric 44

Skookum Cast 32-34

Skunk Ape 36-43, **37**, **40**

  footprints 37

Smith, Marion 4-5

Southwell, Billy 73

Stewart, James 47

Stonin, M.A. 62

Tensing, Lakhpa 48

Titmus, Bob 13, 14, 23, 24

Tombazi, Narik 45

Topilski, Mikhail 62

Waddell, L.A. 45

Wallace, Ray 13, 15, 30, **30**

Wallace, Wilbur 12, 13

Ward, Jennifer 40, **40**

Ward, Michael 44

Westenenk, L.C. 67

Whillans, Don 48

Wildman 6

Yanshow, Li 62

Yeren **6**, 58, 62, **63**

Yeti 6, 44-51, **49**

  fakes 47

  footprints 44-45, **44**, 46, 50

  hands 47, **47**

  newspaper reports about 46

  scalps 46-47, **47**

Yowie 6, 70-75, **71**, **72**, **75**

Zelin, Wang 63

Zhamtsarano, Tsyben 60, 61